# SPIRITUAL CONSCIOUSNESS

# SPIRITUAL CONSCIOUSNESS

BY THE

**VEN. BASIL WILBERFORCE, D.D.**

ARCHDEACON OF WESTMINSTER
CHAPLAIN OF THE HOUSE OF COMMONS
SELECT PREACHER BEFORE THE UNIVERSITY OF OXFORD

GYAN

*Published by*

Gyan Publishing House
5, Ansari Road
Daryaganj, New Delhi-110002
Phone: 011-47034999, 9811692060
E-mail: books@gyanbooks.com

*Distribution Network*
gyanbooks.com
India, USA, Canada, UK, Australia, France



ISBN : 978-81-212-6294-1 (PB)
First Published, 1913

2nd Impression 2022

*Printed at:* Gyan Press, Delhi.



**SPIRITUAL CONSCIOUSNESS**
Author: VEN. BASIL WILBERFORCE, D.D.

# SPIRITUAL CONSCIOUSNESS

BY THE

VEN. BASIL WILBERFORCE, D.D.

ARCHDEACON OF WESTMINSTER

CHAPLAIN OF THE HOUSE OF COMMONS

SELECT PREACHER BEFORE THE UNIVERSITY OF OXFORD

# FOREWORD

The thoughts expressed in the following sermons, by one who is himself only a pupil in the great school of spiritual consciousness, are reproduced in this more permanent form in response to urgent and reiterated requests. For each one who has demanded this reproduction, and for each one who may follow the thoughts with sympathy, the writer invokes, for the coming Christmas and New Year, the following benediction—

Unto God's gracious mercy and protection I commit you; the Lord bless you and keep you; the Lord make His face to shine upon you and be gracious unto you; the Lord lift up the light of His countenance upon you, and keep you consciously abiding in His Presence and in His Peace now and for evermore.

The Lord Almighty bless thee,
  From His own heavenly store;
The fulness of His Presence
  Be with thee evermore.

Exodus xxxiii. 14.

The God of glory keep thee;
  Keep thee in perfect peace;
Lead thee bravely forward,
  Till every conflict cease.

Isaiah xxvi. 3, 4.

# CONTENTS

CONTENTS

# Spiritual Consciousness

## A NEW YEAR

"When He giveth quietness, who then can make trouble?"—JOB xxxiv. 29.

IN other words: No traditional misconceptions rooted in the mind, no credal limitations enforced by mediæval schoolmen, no ingenuities of theological casuists, no intricate "plans of salvation" built out of isolated texts severed from universal declarations, can disturb or overcome the soul that lives in conscious oneness with God, and who knows that inasmuch as "of Him and through Him and to Him are all things," there is no room in this wide universe for the prevailing misbelief in the essentiality and permanence of Evil.

We enter to-day upon yet another of those articulations of Eternity that we call years.

We are obliged to talk to each other in time-conceptions, for in time-conceptions we live. We know not what time is, we cannot even define it. Sir Oliver Lodge calls it "the constant and regular conversion of the future into the past." Another calls it "the mental extension of the present moment into the past and the future." Whatever it is, the first day of a new year reminds us that it creeps ever on. As Barry Cornwall says, "With what a gentle foot doth silent Time steal on his everlasting journey." There is no arresting the silent journey of time, and time is the infant school of the human soul, to which our attention is emphatically challenged to-day.

In what mental attitude are we purposing to meet this New Year, pregnant with its unknown possibilities ? I make a suggestion. It is that we should resolve, here and now, to meet the coming days without a shadow of fear. The fact that we have entered upon this New Year to-day is proof positive that it is one of Abba Father's messages to each one of us. God offers us this New Year ; and the blank sheet laid before us to-day is, as it were, the most recent word to us from our Father Who loves us. Many would much rather not have entered on this year, but He would not have given us the message if it had not been for our highest good. The secret of the quiet mind, the "quietness that He giveth," lies in clearing the imagination from apprehension, and the road to this freedom from fear is to train the conscious mind to rise into its right attitude towards God, and to know ourselves and others after the spirit rather than after the flesh; as individualized expressions, imaginations, thought-children of the Infinite Spirit. In that consciousness of God, in that realization of living in a Presence, we are in His peace, His calm, His quietness. And "when He giveth quietness, who then can make trouble."

Who is this personal pronoun, this "He" who giveth quietness? "He" is the Originating Spirit, the Universal Creative Mind, the Divine Love-force, the Omnipotent imaging power, Who has concentrated all worlds and all life out of His own indefinable, unthinkable substance, and Who is expressing some quality of Himself in all that is. Let us clear our minds of that delusion that God has no consciousness of matter. Matter is not an illusion, it is not unreal, it is divine. God has nothing but His own perfect substance out of which to make worlds; the substance of matter is God. "Earth's crammed with Heaven and every common bush afire with God." The whole creation, with its myriads of planets, suns, and heavens, is full of God. How much more is God in man? and when any human entity, any individual life-centre, in whom Divine Love has expressed Himself, opens his soul inwardly to this inmost divine element, and discovers his true, essential, inseverable relation to the Originating and Indwelling Power, no "trouble" arising from the failure of the physical body, or the wrong thinking of men, or the solicitations of the flesh, or the discipline of life can trouble him, his real self, his inmost being. The surface of his life may be, nay, assuredly will be, often disturbed; he will have his share of weeping, his human self will cry, Eloi, Eloi, but in the sublimest region of his being he will have peace, perfect peace. He knows that there is only one life, and in that life he lives; only one mind, and that mind he shares; only one spirit, and with that spirit he is blended; of him it is true, "Thou shalt hide him privily by Thine own presence from the provoking of all men, Thou shalt keep him secretly in Thy tabernacle from the strife of tongues." He is in conscious oneness with God: and "when God giveth quietness who then can make trouble."

Perhaps the thought arises: if we are to realize this truth of our being in God, we ought to be able to form some mental conception of the nature of the Divine Being, and as pure Spirit, never beginning, He is and must be unthinkable. True, the percipient mind cannot form a mental image of God; that would be to place the Infinite under a limitation; but we can see Him as Moses, figuratively speaking, saw Him, " sheltered by cleft of rock and shadow of hand." As all things that are, are vibrations, modes of motion, of His Spirit, we can know Him by observing the qualities of His self-manifestations; as the apostle puts it, we can know Him " by the things that are made." We know, for example, that He is Life, by the myriad teeming lives in every inch of space. We know that He is Beauty, by the incomparable majesty of sky and stars and clouds and mountains and valleys and flowers and shells and feathers. We know that He is Love, for humanity has recognized Love as the greatest thing in the universe, the highest quality in all the noblest, tenderest, truest specimens of the human race who have been life-centres in whom God has realized Himself. We know that Love is the ruling emotion of our whole nature; we know, therefore, that the nature of the Infinite consciousness, of which we are minute mirrors, must be Love. But we can know God even more accurately. The Infinite Spirit has given us one wholly unmistakeable Specialization, Manifestation, of what He is in

Himself. In the fullness of time He embodied Himself in one individual life-centre, Who so perfectly represented the Divine Intelligence and Love, that of Him it was proclaimed that men " saw the glory of God in the face of Jesus Christ." Pure Spirit, Infinite Spirit, may be, is, unthinkable ; but when this unthinkable Originator, Whom we have discovered to be a necessary logical inference in the phenomena of the universe, in all creaturely life, and in human beings, specializes, embodies His qualities in one perfect human being for our observation, He is no longer unthinkable. In immensity, in infinity, for ever unthinkable ; in character, in quality, in love, in purpose, eminently thinkable, knowable, lovable, in the revelation of the Incarnation. Jesus is the unit of the universe. Jesus is the complete manifestation of the immanent life in all that is. Jesus is the visible embodiment of what the Originating Spirit is in Himself. Jesus is the perfect illustration of the mode of God's Immanence in you and in me. Jesus is the exhibition to the human race of God's ideal of man. Jesus is the promise that the measure and stature of perfect manifestation of God, to which He attained, shall ultimately be fulfilled in all. Jesus, by claiming us as brethren, encourages us to realize our true relation, as individuals, to the Originating Spirit; and the secret of peace lies in using the power of reflection and imagination with which God has gifted us, to grasp and assert this truth till it becomes a real sense-experience; and then, mentally united to the Omnipotent Parent-Spirit in perfect confidence, what room is there for fear! God is all, and all is God, and God is Love, and "When He giveth quietness, who then can make trouble?"

How can this optimistic idealism be brought into practical application on the plane of ordinary experience? It does not appear to harmonize with the facts of life. There is trouble, sore trouble; there are multitudinous sorrows inseparable from human education. There are. But apart from this standard of idealism, even the average Deist has his reply, based upon the incontrovertible axiom, to which logically there is no answer. All that is included in the dark side of life, either is, or is not, part of the universal order of the cosmos, for which the Originating Spirit is primarily responsible. If it is part of the universal order of the cosmos, then it only appears to us to be disorder, chaos, and it must be included in the "all things that work together for good." If it is not part of the universal order of the cosmos, then God is not Infinite, and we are compelled to predicate another creative source, in antagonism to the good God, a dualism which wipes out even Deism and leaves us practically atheists. But the idealist who believes that all is God and God is all, and to whom God is not a problem to be solved, but a Presence to be loved, sees that God's "quietness" resides in the obtaining, by assiduous practice in right thinking, a new quality of mental outlook. The individual who has discovered his real relation, as a thought of God, to the Originating Spirit, finds his relation to things external re-adjusted; his outlook on life is changed; he sees conditions and circumstances on the plane of the real, the eternal, not on the plane of the transient, the phenomenal. The fact is, his method of thinking is reversed. St. Paul calls it "being transformed by the renewing of your mind." A man who is "transformed by the renewing of his mind" is not thinking from the plane of sense-impressions, he is thinking from what St. Paul calls "the mind of Christ," the Parent-mind, the mind of God, Who is thinking in him.

When he is confronted with the dark side of life he mentally retreats into "the secret place of the Most High"; he turns to the central fountain of life, and he says calmly and quietly, "I am spirit, I am one with God, nothing can hurt *me*, the real me; God in me is infinite love, and peace, and wisdom. No 'thing,' or event, or man can make trouble."

This principle, when it becomes a normal attitude of the mind, works in the solution of life's problems. For example: A Deist asks a spirit-taught idealist, in the face of some tribulation, "Where is now thy God?" The Deist is complaining that God, by which term he means an objective world-ruler, does not interfere to prevent wars and mine explosions, and railway accidents, and the many tragedies which darken the sphere of time-perception. The idealist, the man who has found his right relation as an individual to the Originating Spirit, knows that we humans can only come to consciousness of perfection through the instrumentality of the experience of imperfection, and that the facts of life are the schoolmasters of the soul, and that such interference on the part of a world-ruler would utterly frustrate the whole purpose of life's education and stagnate human evolution. A catastrophe—though the general and spontaneous outflow of sympathy and help, which softens and purifies a whole nation under the shock, might almost seem to justify it—a catastrophe is an effect in a divinely arranged cosmic order which is part of the evolutionary law of human life, which law works unfailingly for universal improvement; to suspend this law, even once, by omnipotent interference, would be to obliterate it wholly. All growth in knowledge, all improvement in mechanical ingenuity, all scientific discovery of the secrets of the material world, have originated from some recognized need, or defect, which defect has possibly produced some great catastrophe; and the keener the sensation caused by the catastrophe resulting from the defect, the stronger has been the stimulus to invention, and to investigation of the sequences of natural law, and the greater the security for the future. If an objective world-ruler, from motives of compassion, were to intervene to save men from the results of inattention, or disobedience to recognized laws of nature, it would reduce mankind to a condition of sterile indolence or hopeless uncertainty. It is essential to the progress of science, it is of the utmost educational value, that effects, however painful, should always follow causes. Experience may be a hard school, but it is Abba Father's school. If He had made man automatically perfect from the first like a correct chronometer, man would have been innocent, but he could never have become a moral being. The only school of character is the incontrovertible axiom, that effects must follow causes.

A poor consolation, you say, to broken hearts and bereaved homes. True; but only because we have not yet learnt mentally to live above the plane of the mortal. These husbands and fathers and sons, you say, after some catastrophe, are dead. "Peace, Peace, they are not dead, they have awakened from the dream of life." Blend your mind with the universal mind, and ask the Parent-Spirit if they are dead. Ask the Lord Jesus if they are dead; He would say, "God is not the God of the dead, but of the living. Ye do greatly err."

You might as well ask the Parent-Spirit if He were dead. When divine love has once taught us the truth of cosmic consciousness, and divine Immanence, we know that the Universal Spirit is Himself in the heart and centre of this transient school of pain and sorrow. It is part of God's self-sacrifice entailed by creation. He shares our sorrows. Then though we shed many bitter tears over the loss of loved visible presences, we have His quietness; and "when He gives quietness, who then can make trouble?" We know that all is well, for God is all, and all is God, and God is Love.

I suggest that we should strive to attain to

a clearer, firmer conception of our essential relation as individuals to the universal Parent-Spirit and to a recognition of the supreme fact that the Parent-Spirit seeks to realize Himself, and express His qualities, through the multitude of human beings who are His children.

I do not lay the flattering unction to my soul that we shall any of us greatly affect the facts of the world at large by our realization of this truth, but if we will suffer God's Fatherly thoughts and purposes, which are pulsing through us, to find expression in our several lives, we shall, individually, experience God's "quietness" within, and we shall be centres of God's peace and God's quietness to others, beginning with our homes, our immediate circle. "Be still," then, "and know." Know that your home, and the home of those you love is in God, and that in God we and they "live and move and have our being."

Be just, and kind, and generous, and true, and enduring, because you know that you are commissioned to be a distributor to others of "the Kingdom of Heaven within you." When you are thus mentally claiming and distributing your divine inheritance, no man can "make trouble" for you. You will not see it. You will not even know it. Your mind will be functioning from another plane, the plane of the true, the real, the spiritual. The principle ruling that plane of thought is love. Let love be the predominant thought, motive, impulse, in your life, and all conditions and circumstances will fall into place. Whenever you manifest love you are God-like, for " God is Love."

There will be, ultimately, a perfected humanity, though many centuries may have to roll by first. The day will come when the Originating Spirit will " see of the travail of His soul and be satisfied." One day the prayer of the Incarnate Lord will be fulfilled, " Thy Kingdom come, Thy Will be done on earth as it is in heaven." This final consummation can only come in one way, namely, by the general recognition and acceptance of the fact that man's true life is the life of God in man. When men, and nations, and an entire humanity, are based on this principle, the principle of a common origin, a common divine life, and a common home in God, " the whole earth will be full of the glory of the Lord." There is a hidden chord in every human heart, which, when touched, vibrates in harmony with this universal truth. I have often repeated that stirring incident of the American Civil War, which was told me in the United States. It was on Christmas Day in the year 1864. A regiment of the North, and a regiment of the South, found themselves encamped on either side of the Rappahannock River, where the stream, though deep, was narrow. Every sound between the rival camps was heard; the strains of the military bands as they played opposing national airs, followed by defiant shouts, inflamed the angry passions of those brothers in deadly strife. As the Christmas evening wore on, still and solemn, suddenly the band of the Southern regiment commenced the significant, plaintive strain of "Home, sweet Home." At first there was dead silence, then the Northern band took up the strain, and the two bands softly played it together in the quiet evening air. Every angry word was silenced, every heart was hushed; sweet memories of home and loving hearts flooded in, nothing but the river kept the men from throwing themselves into each other's arms in contrition and shame. An eyewitness says the scene was indescribable; all hearts were thrilled, and tears were seen on every weather-beaten face. A hidden chord was touched and set vibrating in every heart. It was a chord that spoke of home and love and peace and unity. It was just that one touch of God that makes the whole world kin. Why should that chord be a "lost chord," so far as humanity at large is concerned? Why should angels and the Archangels, and all the company of heaven, yearning over the world, say, " I have sought, but I seek it vainly, that one lost chord Divine "? I pray that the heavenly guides may not " seek it vainly " in any of us. May the breath of God touch that chord and set it vibrating in every heart. May we, as God's children, fully realize our origin, claim our inheritance, and recognize the brotherhood of humanity. Jesus unfolded to us the secret of our power when He said, " the Kingdom of Heaven is within you." If we will resolve to meet every approach of pain, sorrow, temptation, trouble with that affirmation, firmly reiterated, " the Kingdom of Heaven is within me and within all," we shall be sharers in the " victory that overcometh the world."

O be strong then, and brave; pure, patient, and
true.
The work that is yours let no other hand do.
For the strength for all need is faithfully given
From the fountain within you, THE KINGDOM OF
HEAVEN.

## COMING TO THE HELP OF THE LORD

"Curse ye Meroz, saith the Angel of the Lord, curse ye bitterly the inhabitants thereof" (Why this vituperation from an Angel's lips?); "because they came not to the help of the Lord, to the help of the Lord against the mighty."—JUDGES v. 23.

"TO the help of the Lord," twice repeated. Here is a metaphysical suggestion irradiating life with an entirely new idea of solemnity and responsibility. Then the Lord, the Omnipotent, the Omniscient, does need human help against the mighty. I quote this denunciation from the Old Testament Scripture, while repudiating the language and disowning the sentiment, because I see that it gives expression to a profound Eternal truth which is rarely realized. Infinite Immanent Mind needs our help. In this sphere of sense and time, Humanity is as necessary to God for self-realization, and the evolution of His predestined perfection for all, as God is to Humanity. The world is what it is because men either do not know it, or have forgotten it, or will not conform to it. Many do not know it. I have valued friends in a certain interesting school of thought who decline to bring to bear the healing influences of their methods in the treatment of any illness where doctors, surgeons, or materia medica are used, on the ground that God is Omnipotent, and Omniscient, and God needs no help. From the true philosophy of creation the argument is irrational. They who accept Paul's incomparable definition in Ephesians iv. 6, "There is one God, and Father of all, Who is above all, and through all, and in all," know better. They know that Infinite Immanent Mind has projected itself into the limitations of phenomena, and, though Transcendent, is subject to those limitations. "The creation was made subject to vanity," Paul says, "not by its own will, but by reason of God." "The Creation groaneth and travaileth," he continues, "waiting," what for? For Omnipotent interference from without? No, "waiting for the manifestation of the sons of God." The universe, as we see it and know it, is the result of the transmutation of Infinite Thought into matter.

"The sun, the moon, and the stars,
The seas, the hills, and the plains,

Are not these, O soul, the vision of Him Who reigns;
Is not the vision He, though He be not that which He
seems."

The initial movement which made worlds to be was Thought. The creative imagination of Infinite Mind reaching forth to realize in actual material phenomena qualities latent in Itself, but unmanifested and so unrealizable before worlds were made. Therefore God is in all, realizing Himself in different degrees of consciousness, whether in the experience of a doctor, or the skill of a surgeon, or the soothing power of a drug, or the wheeling of a planet, or the song of a bird, or the perfume of a flower. Now this carries on the thought expressed in several previous sermons. I pleaded with troubled souls to "Acquaint themselves with God, and be at peace." I tried to show how the Christ revelation, in its fundamental aspect, had revealed the Immanence, Accessibility, Lovableness, and perfect Knowableness of God. And more, I tried to show how the Incarnation of God specifically in the One perfect life-centre, Jesus the Christ, and the inseverability of Jesus the Christ from the rest of the human race, had revealed the essential divinity of humanity; that the chasm which objective Deism had imagined to exist between earth and heaven was proved to be illusory, and perfect communion with Infinite Spirit, through the Christ, the Christ-nature in man, specialized in the Historic Christ, was always open to all; that the flashing into the consciousness of this truth, that man is essentially divine, was the Advent, the "coming." of the Christ-spirit awakening the hidden Christ-nature in man, so that we could all pray that petition, "Even so come, Lord Jesus," from the highest plane of knowledge, the knowledge that the historic Christ, the Lord Jesus, stands for the divinity of humanity realized by One, and specialized in One, as the truth of human life for all. Now is that proposition true to us, namely, that each separate human life is the reproduction, in an individuality, of qualities which the Infinite Creative Mind perceives within itself and desires to realize in us; that Infinite Creative Mind has sent Jesus as the full-orbed, perfect specimen, the ideal, of this reproduction; that though in Jesus "dwelleth all the fullness of the Godhead bodily," He is the embodiment of principles that are not peculiar to Him, but universal, and that therefore some of the "fullness of the Godhead" dwells also bodily in us, and that we can, by virtue of the divine source of our humanity, claim oneness with Jesus the Christ? Has that Advent come to us? Are the eyes of our understanding opened? Do we realize our essential oneness with Jesus, the historic Christ, who said, "I am in the Father, and ye in Me, and I in you?"

If we are only beginning to know it, our self-realization is wholly changed. When we look upon ourselves, upon the complex being we each one know as "I myself," we say, what Jacob said to his stone pillow, "Surely the Lord is in this place," in this body of mine, "and I knew it not." "I am a manifestation of God, I am a vehicle of the qualities of God, my highest self is 'not I, but Christ that dwelleth in me.'"

I said there are obstacles to our full, conscious realization of this essential union with Infinite Spirit. We are slaves to the material when we are not in communion with the spiritual, and we cannot live in ceaseless, unbroken communion with the spiritual; the tendency of the human mind is against it; mental traditions and hereditary race beliefs are almost irresistible. I mentioned physical pain, the shock caused by moral evil, and perplexity as to the function of human will; with regard to all of them we are under the dominion of inherited erroneous mental images,

Pain. The belief of millions has been that

pain can only be accounted for by supposing that side by side with the Infinite Originator there has existed from everlasting a self-existent, eternal antagonist to the good God.

Right thinking sees that God is all, and all is God, and God is Love. Right thinking sees that Infinite Immanent Mind is a sharer, not a spectator of pain, that universal immanence implies universal consciousness, and universal consciousness must imply universal sensitiveness, and, though the finite mind cannot wholly grasp it, "in all our afflictions He is afflicted, and the Angel of His presence saves us," and when the Angel of pain comes it is in love, and he says—

Child of earth, I come to prove thee,
Hardly, sternly with thee deal,
Mould thee in the forge and furnace,
Make thine iron tempered steel.

But dear God, without whom not even a sparrow falleth, folds around you the everlasting arms. The tranquil, unostentatious strength with which I have often seen pain endured has been to me not only a rebuke and an encouragement, but the strongest evidence of the immanence of God in man.

Moral evil, cruel wrongs perpetrated, gross breaches of the moral law, these constitute a greater obstacle to the realization of the divinity of humanity in many minds than pain. Pain may often be the instrument of highest good, not so evil. One writes to me: "I can go very far with you but I draw the line at the hideous revelations of the 'White Slave Traffic.'" Precisely, that is, you can be an idealist if you are allowed your pet reservation, and if you are not allowed it you become a Deist; like the prophet Habakkuk, who positively scolded Jehovah in the words, "O Lord, how long shall I cry and Thou wilt not hear, cry unto Thee of violence and Thou wilt not save?" This is precisely an illustration of what I said as to our judgment of an untoward incident depending upon the shock administered to our individual moral sense. The horror of the White Slave Traffic is appalling, the suffering inflicted unspeakable. Apply for a terrible pamphlet, printed only for private circulation, called *The Heart of Hell*; it can be obtained by personal application at 8, Park Mansions Arcade, Knightsbridge. The details are revolting. In point, however, of physical agony it is probably less tormenting than the atrocities of the rubber plantations of Putumayo, or the hideous cruelty to animals, illustrated by that unprecedented case of cruelty to a pit pony. What would you have? You would desire an objective Deity to interfere. The idealist, he who has recognized man's right relation to the Originating Immanent Spirit, knows that human beings can only come to consciousness of perfection through the instrumentality of imperfection, and that the facts of life are the schoolmasters of the soul, and that interference on the part of an Omnipotent World-Ruler would utterly frustrate the whole purpose of life's education and stagnate human evolution. It is absolutely essential to the progress of civilization that effects, however painful, should always follow causes; this is the one incontrovertible axiom in the process of human evolution. But just here comes in the application of that denunciation of the Angel of the Lord which I quoted from the Book of Judges. Infinite Immanent Mind is waiting for our help; He is suffering in His creation, He is waiting for Meroz to "come to the help of the Lord against the mighty," He is waiting for "the manifestation of the sons of God." His purpose is to use the divine activity within man to overcome what we know as evil. How can we thus come to the help of the Lord? Of course, we can fight against these abominations by human law, we can make the way of transgressors hard. In countries where women have the vote, and through the influence of that vote on legislation are able to protect their sex, this evil is minimized. Where, as in the United Kingdom, women have no vote, it is the plain duty of the male voters to protect the women by legislation. Thank God, the public conscience is being aroused; we have already enrolled in the Statute Book enactments for the flogging of the vile procurers and kidnappers of girls; this is good so far as it goes, but it only touches the standard of outward conduct, and it is vengeance rather than prevention. These evils must be checked at their source; they belong to the moral world, the region of Spirit and of Will; they are the result of selfishness and passion, through which God's highest gift of immanent divinity is perverted. These vile pimps and procurers are less culpable than the creators of the demand. It is a question of commerce. In Chicago three million pounds annually are gained by the traffic. It is a law of commerce that a demand creates a supply; it is the demand that must be checked, and the demand can only be checked by the resolute determination of an awakened consciousness of the divinity of humanity to raise the standard of purity and self-control amongst men. We can only overcome evil with good, we can only stop the "groaning of creation" by a manifestation of divine sonship. Sin is the concentration of desire upon some other centre than God. I can only really " come to the help of the Lord against the mighty " by making my individual life a perpetual manifestation of recognized divine sonship. How did Jesus come to the help of the Lord against the mighty ? He had all power ; He, who could raise Lazarus, could have smitten into annihilation Pilate and his crew by the power of His thought. When they brought Him the woman taken in adultery He confounded the hoary-headed hypocrites who brought her by placing the blame on the right shoulders in the words, " Let *him* that is without sin cast the stone," as much as to say, the initiator of this sin is the man, not the woman ; it is fallen men rather than fallen women who should be dealt with ; but He always overcame evil with " the patience of immortal love outwearing mortal sin," by always manifesting divine sonship, by a life lived in habitual concentration upon the real, the divine, the Father in Him, and though He founded no social revolution, He changed the face of the world, and was able to say : " I have finished the work Thou gavest Me to do, I have glorified Thee on the earth." What is needed, in addition to these useful legislative enactments, is that a majority of minds who have received the " Advent," the

Christ consciousness, who have realized that they are vehicles of the self-realization of Infinite Spirit, and that the Lord needs their "help against the mighty," should lift the race out of the dominion of the material, by the witness of their own lives and beliefs and testimonies. And this must begin with individuals, with you and with me. It is for each one of us to live in the recollection that we have been thought into human existence to be reflections, manifestations, vehicles, of God, as if each one was the only human individual in the world.

Are we thus, in daily life, "helping the Lord against the mighty"? Are we helping Him to come into His Kingdom? In ourselves first; there are mighty hindrances there; do we, in ourselves, overcome the natural with the spiritual, the temporal with the eternal, the animal nature with the Christ nature? And in social life, in our dealings with children, servants, friends, do we conquer by the simple might of goodness; by gentleness, forbearance, self-suppression; overcoming the seductions of the world around, as Orpheus, in the legend, overcame the Sirens by still sweeter music? Are we soothing the groaning of creation by manifesting as the sons of God? If not, we are not "coming to the help of the Lord against the mighty."

This leads to the question of the function of the human will. First, have we a will? Not in the sense of self-determinism. The only absolute, unlimited, unconquerable Will is the Will of God, and God, we read, "will have all men to be saved," and we are "predestined to be conformed to the image of the perfect Son." Here, or hereafter, His Will must prevail, as we read in Psalm cx. 3: "Thy people shall be willing in the day of Thy power." But though we have no will in the sense of self-determinism, we have a measure of volition, within the compass of God's omnipotence, the functions of which are of the utmost importance.

Why have we this important measure of volition? Cast back the mind to the dateless past. What is there? Let me express it in a few sentences. First, Infinite Mind, unexpressed, undifferentiated; we can make no mental picture of it, but we know that It Is. Secondly, Infinite Mind thinking, "thought creating," phenomena in which to realize qualities perceptible in Himself. Thirdly, Infinite Mind realizing Himself as life and beauty for a million ages in cosmic phenomena without man. Fourthly, Infinite Mind imaging forth from Himself individual human life-centres in which He might realize His highest quality, namely, Love. Then comes in will and the possibility of sin. Love being the only quality which cannot be mechanical, automatic, as is the cosmic consciousness, the life centres who are to manifest Love must have a measure of volition conferring upon them the freedom to refuse. All this is luminously expressed in Troward's Doré Lectures. This refusal of man to be a vehicle, a manifestor, of God's highest quality, means the concentration of his desires and aspirations upon self instead of God, and the result is sin, selfishness, cruelty, out of which emerge the "white slave traffic," and the atrocities of Putumayo, and the abuse of the animal creation. The fall of man is his fall from consciousness of his divinity, his oneness with Infinite Mind. Separating human life in thought from Divine life is the Fall, and the only true Fall.

As Mr. James Rhoades says in his inspired poem, "O Soul of mine"—

> "Know this, O man, sole root of sin in thee
> Is not to know thine own divinity."

The function, then, of the will in this dispensation is clear. Sin and selfishness come from thinking wrongly. Paul indicates that moral reform will come from thinking rightly. He says: "Be ye transformed by the renewing of your mind." Through thought, habitual right thought, will come restoration. The conscious mind held in concentration upon the fact of oneness with the Infinite Immanent Mind will transform the whole life. The function of the will is to be the centralizing principle of the conscious mind. Conscious mind is put into action by some emotion or desire; the place of the will is to force conscious mind to fix on the power of Divine Immanence, and hold it there. Now that is really the whole secret of spiritual growth. You have prayed the Advent prayer, "Even so come, Lord Jesus," and He has come; He has shown you, at least intellectually, that you are essentially one with Him, that in you there is the Christ Mind. Now make it a sense-experience, think yourself into conscious oneness with that interior principle as the truest fact of your being. Affirm "In me is the Divine Immanence, that is my real self, the Infinite Indweller seeks to realize Himself in me, He desires to think His thoughts in me, and His thoughts are thoughts of gentleness, moral purpose, purity, courage, patience." Then use the Will in holding that thought, keep the conscious mind from wandering away from it; it will not become immediately, by any means, the normal attitude of your life, but it will, while it obtains, dispel all lower impulses and irradiate you with a thrilling consciousness of your oneness with God. As you manifest this, you help to still the "groaning of Creation," and your life will be a ministry; you will have "come to the help of the Lord against the mighty," you are lifting the standard of humanity, and you have found the secret of peace, for "Thou shalt keep him in perfect peace whose mind is stayed on Thee."

## MAKING A FACT OF BEING A FACT OF CONSCIOUSNESS

"Never wouldst Thou have made anything if Thou hadst not loved it."—WISDOM xi. 24.

I SUGGEST the pursuit of an ideal, namely, to make a "fact of being" become a "fact of consciousness," and this by assiduous training of the conscious mind to realize that the only atmosphere in which we truly live and move and have our being is an atmosphere of Infinite Omnipotent Love. That is the fact of being. St. John says, "God is Love." St. Paul says, "Love never faileth." This is the basal axiom of the fact of being. Infinite Creative Spirit is Love. The "urge," the compulsion, that caused Infinite Mind to differentiate Itself into millions of sensitive forms, is Love.

Love is always creative, causative, in every sphere, from the highest to the very lowest. There never has existed thought, word, or deed, worth remembering, that was not caused, generated, by love of some kind, even if it were only desire, or love of some not very worthy aim. No life ever appeared on this planet that did not owe its origin to love, even in its lowest evolutionary form of sexual selection; were it only the scientifically recognized male and female in the metals, or the automatic attraction of pollen to stamen in the loves of the plants. Travel up the scale of organic life to man, and you will find that the primal creative impulse in man is always Love. Some love music, others poetry, others literature, others mechanics, and so on; and, as that love is creative, music, poetry, literature and the rest spring forth. No true work of any kind is done in this world except under the impulse of love, either of itself or love of something that it will bring. That is the meaning of "a labour of love"; where this impulse is absent a man fails because he has "no heart in his work." Obviously there are innumerable stages and varieties of love, from the highest, which is Divine, to the lowest, which is little more than a selfish predominant tendency. The subtlety of the Greek language differentiates between the three main forms of love in three distinct words, for all of which we have but one English equivalent. Agape is the highest, the word used in 1 Corinthians xiii. Philein, to love, is the word used by St. Peter in his reply to the Lord's threefold question, "lovest thou Me?" (our Lord used the highest word, Agape; St. Peter replied only by the use of the more limited word, Philein). And, thirdly, Eros, the lowest form of love, the word from which our expression "erotic" is derived. But whether it be the highest, Agape, or the more limited form expressed by the word Philein, or the lowest, Eros, which is just animal love unregulated by intelligence, or whether it be the lowest of all, lower than Eros, namely, self-love, the utter inversion of the power that made the universe, still the analysis and study of motive forces proves the proposition that love of some kind is the only creative power in the universe. Love, desire, is causative because it is the mainspring of the mental machinery, and everything is a thought before it is a thing. Let your mind dwell on that statement for a moment, for it implies much. "Everything takes form in thought before the thought takes form in the thing." A great Oratorio takes form in the mind of the composer before the thought of the composer takes form in the score. You and I took form in the thought of Infinite Mind before that thought of Infinite Mind took form in you and me. That is the meaning of that cryptic saying in the Book of Wisdom: "Never would God have made anything if He had not loved it." How could He love it before He had made it? He could love it because it had form in His thought, before His thought had form in manifestation. So God loved you and me before we were born into the world, before we became self-conscious individualities. "Never would He have made us if He had not loved us." How clear and perfect an answer does this give to the question, Whence came we? We know logically that thought must have been antecedent to matter. An Infinite Universe implies an Infinite Thinker. Therefore man, the crown of the Universe, has come by thought-generation from the Universal Mind, and had form in that Mind before he had form in body.

But if God loved us as "thought forms" before we were born, why did He not leave us in the womb of His mind, why did He let His thought of us take form in flesh and blood? Because we could never have come to self-consciousness and God-consciousness except through separation; that is why I said that the so-called "Fall" was believing in the possibility of separation from God, and that it must have been fore-ordained. There can be no moral relationship, no loving intimacy, between a mother and her unborn child, except through separation, followed by a period of unconsciousness on the part of the separated offspring, succeeded by a slowly dawning recognition, ultimately giving place to a full, intelligent affection and union between two, who, if they had never thus been separated, would never have consciously come together.

You and I were thus undifferentiated thought-forms in the womb of the creative mind of the Mother-Soul of the Universe. Thus to have remained would have saved us many tears, but it would have been never to have known the unspeakable joy of coming home to God; therefore the "thought" became a "thing," and we were projected into terrestrial birth, that we might know ourselves as personal spirits, and in slowly dawning consciousness recognize our capacity for knowing God even as we have ever been known by Him; and the profound interior compulsion under which the Mother-Soul thus differentiated us into separate entities called individuals was Love, and we are because God loved us, loved us before He made us, and, inasmuch as Love "never faileth," the agency by which Love will gradually advance the moral evolution of that which It has caused to be, must be ultimately irresistible. Yes, ultimately irresistible, because "God is Love," and, "Love never faileth."

Now this wholly sweeps away the old libel of the everlasting loss of souls. That this conception still holds some minds is, of course, due to the lamentable mistranslations in the New Testament. I am frequently confronted, e.g., with Matthew xxv. 46: "These shall go away into everlasting punishment." I can't blame people for taking these words literally, but they are a mistranslation. The Greek words are *colasis aionios*, "the pruning of the age to come." I have been told that at any rate the doctrine is the doctrine of the Church of England. I deny it absolutely. I sadly allow that it could be implied by some of the regrettable Latinisms in our liturgy and formularies, especially from that amalgam of misapplied passages of Scripture torn from their contexts which we are directed to read in the "Commination service" on Ash Wednesday, but it is not *de fide* in the Church of England. In 1562 Convocation solemnly repudiated it; in 1864 the Judicial Committee of the Privy Council gave judgment that it was not a doctrine of the Church of England, and this judgment was given with no recorded protest from the two Archbishops who sat as Assessors. No, God is Love, and Love is God, and "never would He have made anything if He had not loved it," and man's inextinguishable assurance is based on the axiom " Love never faileth."

Love of some kind, as I said, is creative in every sphere, from the propagation of a butterfly to the building of a motor-car. It is even creative in the sphere of dogmatics. Whence came the conception which finally crystallized into the doctrine of the Holy Trinity? It emerged from the conviction that God is Love. In all the ancient religions of the world that were philosophic, such as Eastern religions, a conception of plurality, consistent with perfect unity in the Divine nature, was intuitive. Why? Whence did this conception of plurality arise? To these thinkers the Infinite Mind was conscious of certain qualities in Itself, qualities constituting what we call Love, which qualities could not be actively realized unless expressed in objective phenomena. That there might be an object for love, the Infinite Mind was self-differentiated into multitudes of individual life-centres. We are of course out of our depth because we are finite, but these life-centres are Himself and yet not Himself, as your thought of yourself is one with yourself and yet not yourself. That is as near as we can get. This conception is traceable in the ancient Chaldean religions, it glows in

Zoroastrianism, it is perceptible in the Indian Vedas, and in the Upanishads it is almost a dogma. Unity of essence, with diversity of manifestation and self-realization, in order that Originating Spirit might have something to love, underlies them all. The thinkers of the Christian dispensation, inheritors of the thoughts of the ages, recognized this necessity for differentiation in the self-realization of the Infinite Spirit. Jacob Boehme taught: God is Spirit, and Spirit that is both love and will, but He can only be self-conscious as He comprehends within Himself a difference with Himself that is yet one with Himself, for a unit has nothing in itself that it can will or love. In differentiation in phenomena, Infinite Spirit recognizes Itself, and, without phenomena, no consciousness would be possible. There is little doubt that this subtle philosophic thought built itself into the theological doctrine of the Holy Trinity. The word Trinity is not in Scripture, nor is the doctrine in its fully developed form. The Christians of the second and third centuries had no recognized doctrine of the Trinity. It was not fully established till the year 325, when Athanasius fought the Arians at the Council of Nicæa, and gave us nearly the whole of the beautiful Nicene Creed, but the thought behind it was always there. God is Love, Love regarded as a soleity, an abstraction, apart from an object, is unthinkable. Love is not love if there be no beloved. Love only becomes thinkable in relations, in process, in act. It is therefore obvious that, whatever Infinite Mind might have been antecedent to phenomena, and it is idle to speculate as to that, there never could have been a time when Infinite Mind was not, in a sense, Father. And Eternal Sonship, or the self-realization of God in individual lives, specialized, manifested in the individual life of the Lord Jesus Christ, is not as of succession in time, but as the necessary correlation of Eternal Fatherhood. And the proceeding, creative, suffused, sustaining life of this realized union, as Holy Spirit, became essential to any right thought of Deity. From this conception theologians, always craving for metaphysical definitions, built the dogma of the Holy Trinity. Infinite Love in unthinkable origin was called God the Father. Infinite Love in creative expression, and perfect manifestation in the Lord Jesus, was called God the Son. Infinite Love in universal interpenetration, in Infinite Immanence, and in Eternal procession, was called God the Holy Ghost, and these three are inseverably one, while differentiated in operation.

Now I am told by the unco-orthodox that it

is dangerous thus to accentuate the Love of God and omit His other attributes lest men should reckon too much upon the indulgence of the Almighty. Love is not one of God's attributes, it is Himself, but let that pass. Did it ever occur to these cavillers that the only element in the Divine nature to fear is the inexorableness, the perfection, of His Love? It is at once the glory and the awfulness of the Creative Love that it is irresistible, it "never faileth." The one everlasting impossibility to man is to elude the Love of God. Anger might possibly be propitiated. Outraged justice might accept satisfaction and apology. Love cannot be propitiated or cajoled and does not cool down. "Love never faileth," and will irrevocably and irresistibly fulfil its purpose. Assuredly there is here an aspect of our relation with God calculated to arrest the attention. Are we responding to this Infinite Love? "If thy hand offend thee cut it off," cried the only human being who perfectly knew God. "It is better for thee to enter into life maimed, than having two hands to go into Gehenna, into the fire that never shall be quenched." Though this orientalism is highly figurative, this consuming fire can never be quenched because it is the fire of Love, and "many waters cannot quench Love." And it is only Love, absolutely perfect Love, that has strength of purpose to carry through the ultimate remedial operations which may be necessary for the salvation of the wilfully impenitent.

It is only perfect Divine Love, immanent and transcendent, that can go into Hades with Dives, and purge him from the flesh accretions that have drugged his conscience, and smothered his spiritual being.

It is in the current of this ultimately resistless stream of Divine loving purpose that our lives are placed, and it is well to recognize it. What our Lord calls " cutting off the right hand " is a strong figure of the use of our will in compelling the obedience of the body. " I keep under my body," says Paul. We humans, though one in essential life, differ in our personal equations as widely as leaves on trees. I cannot prescribe for you, or you for me, what hand must be cut off, what eye plucked out.

One thing is certain. Divine Love will instantly work with us when we begin to be receptive to His Love. First, because we are " predestined to be conformed to the image of the Perfect Son." Nothing can ultimately thwart that predestination, and Immanent Spirit will fly to meet our co-operation. Secondly, because the Kingdom of Heaven, the potentiality of the Christ character, is within us at this moment. "Dwelt no power Divine within us, how could God's Divineness win us?"

> "Not vaulted arch nor dome Thy glories span,
> Thy habitation is the heart of man.
> This ancient shrine is Thy most holy place,
> Where Thou dost meet Thy children face to face.

St. Paul tells us that the process of making a "fact of being a fact of consciousness" is by "renewing of our mind." "Change your thinking," he would say. Paul reminds us that we have a carnal mind, we know it well, a habit of thinking full of fear and resentment and selfishness. We inherited it, and we have added to it; it is always persuading us that present consciousness and material conditions are permanent and real. We have also, he says, the "mind of Christ." This is the real self, our link with the Infinite, the mind which is God within us. The question is, will I force my conscious mind to turn towards this inner mind, this spirit mind? Will I, by assiduous practice, make this fact of being a fact of consciousness, learn to know myself not after the flesh, but after the spirit, and thus become free from the delusions, the sense experiences of that part of me which is not my true self. Paul says we can arrive at this self-knowledge, and obviously he attained to it himself.

This is not something that we have got to become, it is to recognize something that we already are. It is a question of mental self-treatment. It is compelling the conscious mind at certain times to realize vividly the indwelling Presence, and then, speaking to Infinite Love. " Infinite Father Spirit, thou art in me, I desire that Thou wilt fulfil Thy highest thoughts in me unhindered by my carnal mind. Thou art desiring to love through this heart of mine with Thine own tender love which ' thinketh no evil, endureth all things, beareth all things '; I wish to yield, with full receptivity, to Thy desire to realize Thyself as Love in me."

Then begin to put it into practice. Are you prejudiced against any one ? Mentally ask forgiveness of that one. Have you spoken against any one unkindly, or criticized them ? Mentally withdraw your words, ask them, in the silence of your own heart, to forgive you.

Determine to see everybody, however objectionable in outward form, as pure spirit; and if there are people that you dislike, send them your strongest thoughts of love, say " that person is God's child." Then, after a mental self-treatment of this kind, go forth again to your ordinary life, acknowledging the all-loving indwelling Presence as the sole motive-power of your actions. Use your will to keep in the spirit of recollectedness that Infinite Mind dwelling in you desires you to be patient, loving, kind, self-suppressing in all circumstances. While this attitude is maintained you will be thinking from the Christ Mind, you will be living on the plane of the real, and your subconscious mind, that little understood "sympathetic system," will adopt the suggestion, and will build and externalize these thoughts into character, and we shall be spiritually growing, and on the way to the attainment of the attitude which can say with Paul, who had made his fact of being a fact of consciousness, "I live, yet not I, but Christ liveth in me."

## RESURRECTION

" I will destroy this Temple made with hands, and in three days I will build another made without hands. [And St. John, referring to this incident, says] : " He spake of the Temple of His Body."—St. MARK xiv. 58.

IT is not easy to stray from conventional lines on Easter Day, the glorious Festival is so bound up with traditional beliefs and emotions. Personally I am content to be filled with Luther's thought, when, in his prison cell, he wrote with his fingers in the dust, again and again, just the words " vivit vivit, He lives He lives." Yes, He lives, Jesus lives, the same Jesus, the Jesus " Whom having not seen we love." But we shall see Him; " when we wake up after His likeness, we shall see Him as He is."

The absorbing thought of to-day is Resurrection, and, though we may hold different conceptions as to the meaning of the word Resurrection, there is one thing it means to all, namely, continuity of individuality, utter abolition of death as a concrete reality, the exposure of death as a sham and a delusion.

It is mere self-deception, of course, to pretend that death is a delusion on the physical plane; it is not; it is still the "last enemy," hateful in its details, and a cruel separator of loving presences. But, remember, death is also the re-uniter of loving presences, the welcome concluder of periods of utter loneliness. There is an attitude, some here know it, which says: "Welcome, dear death, welcome; come when you please, and as soon as you please, offensive as you are in your details, welcome; for when you come you will re-unite those whom once you separated."

The inference from the manifested survival of the Representative of the race, which is the message of Easter Day, is the assurance afforded that death is but "the suburb of the life Elysian," for Jesus stands for the race, and "He showed Himself alive to above five hundred brethren at once."

Now this "showing Himself alive," what does it imply? There are two things it does not imply; it affords no argument for the old belief in the reconstitution of our flesh bodies, and it provides no analogy of the ordinary condition of disembodied humanity. His appearances during the forty days were exceptional manifestations, obviously intended to convince His disciples of the continuity of His individuality. They were what are now called "materializations," constantly differing and gradually becoming more and more etherealized, until, at the last appearance on the mountain of Galiliee, some were unable to recognize Him. These materializations prove the deathless endurance of the ego, and that, in certain exceptional circumstances, a discarnate spirit can mentally concentrate the surrounding ether into a temporary materialization that is recognizable. Spencer says—

> "For of the soul the body form doth take,
> For soul is form and doth the body make."

But soul is mind, and mind, remember, is creative.

Now if our Lord did say, as it is almost certain He did say, "I will destroy this body, and in three days I will build another," He gave the answer to a question constantly asked, namely, What became of the body, born of Mary, which was laid in the tomb? It is perfectly obvious that our Blessed Lord rose not out of any tomb, but out of the body which He left hanging on the Cross, and from thence He Himself went direct to Hades, that He might minister to the Spirits of those who were drowned in the Flood

Therefore, He Himself never entered the sepulchre in which His body was laid. The question then arises, What became of His Body? He is reported to have said, "I will destroy this body"; in other words, "I will dematerialize it, disintegrate it, resolve it into its constituent elements." Not by miracle. but by perfect knowledge of a natural law which is not yet cognized by Science, but which, quite possibly, will sooner or later be brought under scientific control to the abolition of the horror of corruption. It was specially prophesied of His body, you remember, that it should not see corruption, it was to be disintegrated by the process which Paul says will obtain with regard to those who will be on the planet when it is destroyed. "They shall be changed," St. Paul said, "in a moment, in the twinkling of an eye." Then our Lord said, "I will build another body." That expression could not refer to the glorious spiritual enswathement which John saw at Patmos. That was His glorious Body, the Body in which He is now, and in which we shall see Him. "I will build." That is He materialized, by thought-power, from the condensed atoms of the ether, these appearances, which were different on each occasion, as His thought of Himself differed. On Easter morning He was apparently clad as a Galilean vine-dresser, so that Mary mistook Him for the gardener; another time He was unclothed and with wounds; again St. Mark tells us "He appeared to two of them on the road to Emmaus in another form." These materializations then do not suggest the reconstitution of the flesh body, an ingrained hereditary race-belief originating from the Egyptian religion. Obviously Infinite Creative Mind could, if He pleased, recall the disintegrated atoms of the particular body in which we each one die, from the multitude of changes through which these atoms would have passed, and rebuild them around our souls and spirits, though considering the number who have used these particles, there would not be enough to go round, and to allot them to their separate tenants would be a greater miracle than the creation of the world. But the fact is that Scripture nowhere tells us that our physical bodies shall rise again. Where texts appear to lend colour to this view, they are almost invariably mistranslated, either accidentally or purposely. Sometimes purposely. After the Council of Nicæa, A.D. 325, the Scriptures were tampered with to a great extent. Professor Nestle, in his introduction to *The Textual Criticism of the Greek New Testament*, tells us that certain scholars called in Greek "διορθωταί," or in Latin *correctores*, were appointed by the ecclesiastical authorities and actually commissioned to correct the text of Scripture in the interests of what the Church considered orthodoxy. Even when these mistranslations are accidental they are difficult to abolish. For example, that text from Job xix., painfully familiar to our ears, always connected with bereavement, "I know that my Redeemer liveth, and though after my skin worms destroy this body, yet in my flesh shall I see God," distinctly implies the resurrection of the flesh. Now it has long been known that in the orginal language it is exactly the contrary. The right translation is, "Though after my skin this body be destroyed, yet without my flesh I shall see God." And yet, though a partial correction is placed in the margin of the R.V., we continue, at every funeral service, to repeat the old error. So strong are hereditary race-beliefs.

No, the promise of God is the permanence of the individuality, not the resurrection of the body. "Thy brother," says the Lord Jesus to Martha, "shall rise again." "To-day," He said to the penitent thief on the cross, "shalt thou," the conscious being, the real man, the individual with thought, memory, and will, "shalt thou be with Me in Paradise";

the body of that malefactor would have been burning in the valley of Himmon at the very time when Jesus was taking him, his individuality, to Paradise. In the parable of Dives and Lazarus we read that the "beggar died and was carried," not a part of him, but his entire self, "was carried by the angels into Abraham's bosom." Paul is full of contempt for those who imagine that the flesh body will rise. "Thou fool," he says, "thou sowest not that body that shall be." He implies that whoever has sown a seed and watched it grow, knows that that which comes up is not that which was sown; the outer portion of the seed dies, putrefies, mingles with the earth, but from within arises the green, vivid shoot, moving mountains.

Thank God, we shall say good-bye to our body for ever. When it has done its work it dies, decays, putrefies, mingles with the elements around and there is an end of it, till its particles form part of another body; but from within, the man, the real man, rises into the new conditions, the other dimension, not out of the grave, but out of the body. The moment of death is the moment of resurrection, the essential identity the same, the sensible materials changed; the same corporeal individuality, not the same integral atoms.

One stronghold of the materialistic conception of resurrection is our attitude towards human bodies after death. Half the epitaphs on tombstones, and most of our funeral hymns, are sheer materialism. I grant that devotion to a beloved body is an irresistible instinct. Nothing can be more natural than that we should cling to that shell that we have cherished, upon which we have lavished our affection. Natural, yes, but not Spiritual! It savours of mentally identifying them with the body, and ignoring the survival of individuality apart from the body. When we realize that resurrection is not a return to flesh life, like the recalling into his body of the spirit of Lazarus, or the sending back into earth conditions of the widow's son of Nain; when we realize the fact that the departing spirit finds itself enswathed by a brighter, better, clothing, not made of the grosser matter which we now animate, then we shall be better able to withdraw our attention from the worn-out chrysalis, and mentally follow the beloved into the other dimension.

Personally, whilst I recognize the grave difficulty in connection with poison, I welcome cremation as a valuable protest against identifying the individual with the body, as inculcating the true view of resurrection as taught by Our Lord when He argued with the Sadducees that

Abraham, Isaac and Jacob were risen, as much as they ever would rise, though their bodies were still in the grave.

Then, again, these materializations of Our Lord afford no argument whatever in favour of that, to me, utterly repulsive conception of eschatology called re-incarnation; the theory that we shall be re-embodied on this planet again and again until the *manas*, the higher mind, has learnt to gravitate towards the Spiritual ego. If this doctrine were true, life, to me, would not be worth living, I should wish I had never been born. I should say to Creative Mind—

> " Wherefore from silent earth
> Didst Thou awake and curse me into birth ? "

Imagine being mechanically doomed to countless re-births in the " vile body," with a fresh personality and probably a different sex each time, wandering with the curse of Cain upon your brow, suffering, in a totally different personality, for sins committed in some previous existence which you have utterly forgotten. The conception is hateful, irrational, an absurd contradiction of the law of evolution, and the utter destruction of personal immortality, for to be reincarnated with no memory of your former self is to be a new soul. It is difficult to trace the origin of this widespread superstition.

It is certainly not in the primitive Eastern faiths

In the earliest Veda, the Atharva Veda, probably the oldest record in the world, there is no hint of Reincarnation, and full belief in personal immortality. You read: " Conduct us to heaven, O Lord, where our friends dwell in bliss, having left behind the infirmities of the body for ever, and where the wife shall be united to the husband." No, this incarnation is our only flesh and blood infant school. Other schools, if needed, will be in other conditions. Can you imagine the prodigal son, after a restful time in Devachan with his ring and his fatted calf, being sent back to the harlots and the swine husks to work out his Karma without even the safeguard of remembering his past experiences ?

Now assuming the hypothesis, which to me is more than a hypothesis—to me it is God's truth —that resurrection, anastasis, does not mean the reconstruction of my flesh and blood body; that when I say in the Creed, " I believe in the resurrection of the body," I mean, in the universal sense, the continuity of the whole body of humanity, for humanity is the Body of God, and in the particular sense, the anastasis or uprising of the spiritual body from the corpse at the moment of death, a further important consideration arises. What is this spiritual body? I risk being called a fool by St. Paul for asking the very question which he derides: "With what body do they come?" There must be a body, a form. Tennyson was right when he said—

> "Eternal form shall still divide
> Eternal soul from all beside,
> And I shall know him when we meet."

Substance, form, of some kind, are essential to the manifestation of spirit. Originating Spirit required substance and form for His self-realization, and acquired it in the Cosmos. Individual spirit also must have some concrete form. This form, this clothing, is what Paul refers to when he says: "There is a natural body and there is a spiritual body." "There is," not "there shall be." So this ethereal, non-atomic enswathement, not subject to the limitations of matter, called the spiritual body, is within us now. Inasmuch as thought is creative, and, as Spencer says, "Of the soul the body form doth take," we are building, weaving, thought-forming this body, so far as its moral qualities are concerned, every day we live. It will be the expression of our conception of ourselves, and of our relation to Infinite Mind. A spiritual body, an ethereal enswathement of spirit, the moral qualities of which are woven by a mind humbly striving to be conscious of its oneness with Infinite Mind, will be perfectly adapted to the greater life and experience which will open to us when we pass over. But it may be otherwise; we may be resisting the automatic striving of the Christ within us, we may be building an enswathement which is deriving its moral qualities and forming its character only according to the carnal promptings of this world, and what then? There is an allusion in the Apocalypse to "the second death." What is the second death? Whatever it is, we know that Eternal Love will preside over the process, and the second death will destroy nothing but that which excludes the soul from the higher privileges; but what is it? It cannot be physical, for the physical body is gone; it cannot be death of the spirit, for "The spirit shall never cease to be never." It must be the process in which a wrongly formed enswathement of spirit is cast off in the next world. It must be the fulfilment of the saying, "The soul that sinneth it shall die," not the spirit, the spirit cannot die. The important question is, From what centre within me is my soul now deriving its qualities and forming its character? Have I given, by my thought-power, an Easter

Day, a resurrection, to the Christ within me? Do I know "the power of His resurrection" within me? I do not mean, Am I perfect? We shall not attain sinless perfection here, Paul said he had not attained. "If I might attain," he said, "to the resurrection," meaning the full resurrection of the Christ within him, "not as though I had already attained or were already perfect." Do I know that the Christ within me, the Divinity, is waiting to be recognized, acknowledged, liberated, resurrected? Am I desirous of co-operating with Him in the steady, gradual conquest of the lower life by the higher? Then, though I am far from perfect, all is well, for the Christ within me has had His Easter, and has risen from the grave of my lower nature in His Majesty and Power. "Blessed and holy is he that hath part in the first resurrection," and the first resurrection is the resurrection of the Christ in you, "On such the second death hath no power."

Finally, if you have resurrected the Christ within you, your duty in life is just beginning. "Come to the help of the Lord against the mighty." Be a builder of the spiritual nature in others, resurrect the Christ in others. The Christ is buried in living tombs of human individualities more surely than ever He was in Joseph of Arimathea's grave, indeed, He never was in that sepulchre. The gravestone of the carnal nature lies on thousands of buried Christs. When you, by your example, your manifestations of love, your radiation of some soul-quality from your consciousness of God, bring new thoughts of light and life to the soul of another, you have given the indwelling mystic Christ an Easter, a resurrection, in that heart. Oliver Wendell Holmes uses that very simile in his book, *The Autocrat of the Breakfast Table.* He is speaking of lifting a stone in a field, a thing we have often done, and revealing creeping things and blanched herbage and faded grass. " Lift the stone," he says, " and next year you will find the grass growing tall and green where the stone lay; whoever puts the staff of truth to the old lying incubus, lifts the stone, then shall the true nature which has lain blanched and broken rise in its full stature."

That is what you will have accomplished when you have lifted the stone of carnality, of wrong thinking, from some brother's heart, and resurrected the Christ in him; when you have helped another to overcome the bondage of sin and death in his soul by " the power that worketh in him." This is indeed to realize your true relation to the Originating and Indwelling Spirit, and " to come to the help of the Lord against the mighty."

## THE HOLY SPIRIT

"The Spirit of Jesus."—ACTS xvi. 7, R.V.

THESE four words clear my own mind from the confusions which have arisen from the lust for metaphysical definition which has infected all organized Churches from the earliest times. The tendency presumably arose from the desire of ecclesiastics to protect what measure of truth they possessed by enclosing it in verbal propositions and dogmatic definitions to be used as tests for the extinction, by penalty, of what they considered unorthodoxy.

There must, of course, be words in which to express thoughts, but it should always be taken into consideration that the phraseology of earth-life is inadequate to express, in any final form, the realities and infinities of Spirit-Life, and this fact must confront all who, like myself, have to speak on Whit Sunday. The conventional conception of the Holy Ghost as a separate and distinct Divine Person is a growth, it was not a belief of early Christianity.

There is no trace of it at the time of the compilation of our Apostles' Creed, which, though substantially Apostolic, dates, in its present form, from about the middle of the second century. Professor Harnack, of Berlin University, perhaps the greatest theological historian of our day, affirms that the latter part of the Nicene Creed, which was added at the Council of Constantinople, forty-four years after the Council of Nicæa, is not meant to imply that the Holy Ghost was in any sense a separate Person, but an afflatus, an influence, an outflowing operation of the Divine Self-consciousness.

The words, "The Spirit of Jesus," convey to my own mind all the conception I need. God, Infinite Mind, is Spirit. God's Self-contemplation, His thought of Himself, is the Logos. The Logos, the self-contemplation of Infinite Mind, was "made flesh and dwelt among us," and Jesus was the "flesh" that the Logos was "made." So the Holy Ghost is the afflatus of Infinite Mind, qualified with a new conception of "personalness" acquired by specialization in Jesus, and justifiably spoken of under a new name since the Incarnation, as "the Spirit of Jesus."

Shall we follow out that thought? God is

Spirit, Spirit is undefinable, Spirit is the Thought-power which has differentiated itself into the millions of specific visible forms. Spirit is an Infinite Unity, therefore the distinctions which obtain between one specific visible form and another, vast as they are, such as the distinction between a man and a microbe, or the distinction between ourselves and an Archangel, are distinctions of degree and not of kind, and behind all distinctions is a profound essential unity which supports every form into which Spirit has expressed Itself, according to its place in the cosmic order; so, as God is Infinite, and there cannot be two Infinites, we are justified in saying: " Elementally, God is all and all is God." What, then, do we mean when to-day, on the Festival of the Holy Ghost, we say, in the Constantinople end of the Nicene Creed, " I believe in the Holy Ghost, the Lord, the Life-giver " ? Are we unorthodox if we form our own mental conception of this " Lord and Life-giver," theologically called the Holy Ghost ? We can accept the theological expression as a convenient verbal accommodation, but if it is to be a vital truth to us our thoughts must be unhampered.

We may think of Spirit under two aspects, the universal and the particular, as regards His Immanence as Cosmic Consciousness in the visible world, and as regards His Self-expression in individual human beings. In the universal, the cosmic sense, Spirit is the Originating and reproducing energy out of which all forms of existence emerge, the ceaseless activity of the Divine Mind, expressing itself in and sustaining all forms of life, and the whole of this wonderful universe, earth and sky, and sun and stars, and mountains and rivers, and plants and animals, are expressions of Spirit. This diffused, universal aspect of Spirit is sometimes contemptuously called Pantheism, but, Pantheistic or not, it is peace to know that we are penetrated and ensphered by God. It is glorious to know that God is not an objective Despot to be feared, but a Divine Presence to be found and loved everywhere. To think of it in the solemn hush of a starlit night, is to be fortified with the consciousness that your minute, almost microscopic, individuality, is grandly enfolded in the irresistible purpose of Omnipotence. It freshens the conviction that the " Earth is the Lord's " to recognize Him as the stimulating force in all that tends to beautify and to brighten human life ; to know that all that is noblest in art, all that is deepest and truest in poetry, literature and science, is Divine Self-consciousness expressing Himself in diversity of manifestation. The suggestion that matter has no reality is scattered to the winds by this affirmation.

The Old Testament conception of Spirit was almost confined to material force and intellectual and bodily gifts. The Spirit is declared to be the abnormal physical power even in a debauched Hercules like Samson. Being a lover of precious stones myself, I rejoice to be assured that the first polisher of gems was inspired for the purposes of his craft by the Spirit. We read of Bezaleel, the son of Aholiab, that he was filled "with the Spirit, in all manner of workmanship, in gold and silver, and the cutting of stones." The Old Testament conception of the Spirit, though it differs from modern orthodox definitions, is a valuable protest against the banishment of the presence of God from any department of His universe, and it strengthens the conviction that beneath the bewildering complexity of the world's life, Spirit "shapes our ends, rough-hew them how we may."

But what is the significance of Pentecost, of Whit Sunday, in connection with our mental conception of Spirit? I look upon that scene in the upper chamber at Jerusalem as an instance of an historic happening intended to accentuate a spiritual truth. The incident of Pentecost with its tongues of fire, and miraculous gifts, is rather on Old Testament lines, but taken in connection with our Lord's own words, in which He more than hinted that Pentecost was His own second coming, it helps us to think "Personalness" into that which is Infinite, a Personalness justifying individual intercourse with It.

This "Personalness" added to the thought-image of Spirit is "the Comforter." Pantheism, after all, leaves one cold. When one has been in physical pain, or crushed under some bitter sorrow, I do not know that one ever gets much comfort from the knowledge that the vast solitudes of nature are quivering with Spirit. It is rather the cold, silent, unsympathizing beauty of the great god Pan, for there are no moral qualities in nature; life and beauty in profusion, but not Love, as we understand it. The sense of want of moral consciousness in Immanence is partially relieved by the knowledge that the Spirit is self-conscious in humanity in a sense far higher than His self-realization in nature, and man is conscious of moral qualities. In that fact lies our responsibility for striving to live *to* the Spirit, *in* the Spirit.

"Dwelt no power Divine within us,
How could God's Divineness win us?"

Whenever we have felt a yearning for a purer, better life, it has been God's Divineness appealing from without, to the power Divine within us.

But to be able to think the character of Jesus, the gentleness and compassion of Jesus, into the Holy Ghost, to consider It as the "Spirit of Jesus," is to read into the World-Soul the highest conception of moral qualities; this is to recognize in the silent solitudes of nature that thrilling promise, "I am with you always to the end of the age"; it is to take all the coldness out of Pantheism, and to feel that the Presence is alway a "Jesus Presence."

Dogmatic phraseology has confused us into the idea that there are three separate Individualities in the Godhead.

There are not.

"Hear, O Israel, the Lord our God is one Lord." But the one Spirit specialized His thought of Himself, called the Logos, in the individual life-centre called Jesus, that we might attribute personalness and moral qualities to Omnipresence, and the Holy Ghost, the outflowing Influence of Infinite Mind, and the Logos is unequivocally identified with Jesus.

It is as though the All-Father had said, Spirit is not to be to you an impersonal *anima mundi*, an unapproachable World-Soul with which you can have no conscious dealings. An aspect of personal tenderness has been communicated to it by identifying it with the Lord Jesus, and you may think of the Holy Spirit as the "Spirit of Jesus." Indeed you would be justified in saying Jesus is Infinite Spirit manifested in the flesh, the Holy Ghost is Jesus manifested in the spirit. This identification of the Pentecostal Holy Ghost with the Lord Jesus is the clear testimony of Jesus Himself. "I will not leave you comfortless, I will come to you," He said. It is the testimony of St. Paul, "The Lord" (i.e. the Lord Jesus) "is that Spirit." The identification of the Holy Ghost with the Spirit of Jesus is unmistakable in the Acts of the Apostles, where in the Revised Version it is spoken of as the "Spirit of Jesus." Thus when I say "I believe in the Holy Ghost, the Lord, the Life-giver," I do not mean I believe in a third Individuality in the Godhead, but I believe in the mystic Immanence, the strengthening power, the appealing influence, the perpetual presence of Spirit possessing the moral qualities It manifested when It was specialized in the Lord Jesus. So "the Holy Ghost the Comforter" is the most recent revelation of the Originating Spirit, enabling us mentally to conceive of the cosmic consciousness, the World-Soul, as possessed of personalness, moral qualities, and responsibility, encouraging us to talk to It at all times and in all places as a man would talk to his closest friend. Thus what we call the Trinity is diversity of manifestation, Originating Life, Manifested Life, Outflowing Life, but the same Spirit, and possessing the same qualities in each manifestation, and we may speak of the Holy Ghost as " the Spirit of Jesus."

This conception of universal Spirit as identified with the Lord Jesus, is full of peace and power. It brings back God into His world from which the limitations of objective Deism, and the vagaries of one prominent and increasing school of modern thought, have banished Him, and it brings Him back, not as an impersonal cosmic force, but as such an one as Jesus. It affirms that the world is ruled by personal self-conscious Spirit, not by automatic urge. It adds dignity to the commonest processes of this beautiful planet to know that the constraining motive of the Soul of the Universe is Love, and such Love as was manifested in Jesus. It sustains you when the heart grows faint with the strife of wills and the problem of pain and evil. It is a sunburst of optimism to know that there is no chance, no mere machinery, but everywhere purpose, Love, intelligence, and that the Infinite Mind in operation is the " Spirit of Jesus."

What then is the appropriate mental exercise for Whitsun Day? It is this. To remember that each individual life-centre, present in this church, is one amongst the multiplicity of units into which the Spirit of Jesus has differentiated itself. Therefore the highest mental act of which any individual life-centre is capable is strenuously to think himself beyond the environment of his flesh and blood personality, and realize that he is essentially elementally one with Infinite Spirit. Then inasmuch as Infinite Spirit, undifferentiated, which is God outside you, is immediately responsive to differentiated spirit, which is God within you, we realize the true position of prayer, and can become a healing power in intercession by mentally holding the cases in which we are interested into the Presence of the Supreme Source of all being with eager, loving wish for their welfare even if we speak no words.

Again, inasmuch as the Immanence of God in humanity is "the Spirit of Jesus," or as Paul calls it "Christ in you," this knowledge is a powerful stimulus to the instinct of rescue. The objective personality, Jesus, said, "Go and tell My brethren that I go to My Father and their Father." Go and tell them, so far as you know it yourself, that though they are living in darkness and ignorance, they have that within them that was in the thought-womb of Infinite Mind before the world was, and that God is desiring to realize Himself in their individual lives.

Are there in London any who have never been told that they have an unborn divine self within them to which the Lord Jesus alluded when He said, "My Father and your Father"? Do you remember my telling you of the experience of one of those devoted missionaries who are ceaselessly labouring amongst the outcast? He said to a dying girl in a repulsive London slum, "Do you know about the Lord Jesus Christ?" "No," replied the girl; and she added—and it is difficult to repeat it without tears—"No, I never heard of Him; Who is He? I know He don't live down this court." The blame for that ignorance rests not upon her, but upon the social conditions which make possible such an environment as that in which she lived. It is in such environments that the representatives of the Bishop of London's Fund are working, wiping tears from faces, fighting to remove stumbling-blocks from lives, smoothing the path of the needy and the careworn, finding the hidden Christ in human hearts. The Bishop of London's Fund is God's rescue brigade in this great city, and the very least all can do who are unable to contribute personal service is to give liberally to this organization which is nobly meeting the modern problem of the crowded centres of the population, supplying clergy, building mission-rooms, providing Scripture readers, training deaconesses, building and enlarging churches. The measure of the usefulness of this most valuable agency can only be in exact proportion to the generosity of London churchgoers.

I desire to-day to remind myself and you that this revelation of Pentecost is yours and mine. The Spirit is Infinite, mysterious, undefinable, but It is, as to moral qualities, such an one as Jesus. The Spirit, "the Spirit of Jesus," pleads with our hearts. That gentle voice, "soft as the breath of even," is the Jesus voice, and it whispers, "Know ye not that your bodies are temples of the Holy Ghost?" "Know ye not that the Spirit of God dwelleth in you?" "He that is joined to the Lord is one spirit"; you are meant to be a vehicle of the Spirit, a distributor of the Spirit; Infinite Mind is seeking to realize Himself, and manifest Divine Love in you and through you.

Are we thwarting, grieving, the Spirit? He says, "My Spirit shall not always strive with man." That is, a character hardened by continual resistance to "the Spirit of Jesus" during our education here, can only be unmade by the process which Browning calls " the sad, sequestered state where God unmakes but that He may remake the soul He else had made in vain."

We can always know how far we are living from the Spirit. The test is clear. " The fruit of the Spirit," we are told, " is love, joy, peace, long-suffering, gentleness, self-control."

Are we conscious of these qualities ? Have we manifested any of them during this past week in family life, in social life, in business life, in pleasure life ; in the patient endurance of physical pain, and mental worry ? Remember, " he that hath not the Spirit of Christ," meaning, of course, he in whom " the Spirit of Jesus " has been unrecognized, undeveloped, silenced, thwarted, " is none of His " ; that is, he is living on the lower plane of consciousness. Let us pray, with strong inward intention—

> " Come, Holy Ghost, our souls inspire,
> And lighten with celestial fire.
> Keep far our foes, give peace at home,
> Where Thou art guide no ill can come."

## TRI-UNITY OF FUNCTION. UNITY OF ESSENCE

"No man cometh unto the Father but by Me."—JOHN xiv. 6.

"No man cometh unto Me except the Father draw him."—JOHN vi. 44.

"No man can say that Jesus is the Lord but by the Holy Ghost."—1 COR. xii. 3.

IT is not inappropriate to have three texts on Trinity Sunday. As Paul tells Timothy to "pay attention to doctrine," we may ask how did the doctrine of the Trinity become an article of the Christian Faith? It is always interesting to trace the growth, and ultimate emergence into crystallized shape, of theological dogmas incorporated into the creeds of Christendom.

Before the Council of Nicæa, A.D. 325, there was no definite doctrine of the Trinity. Spiritual thinkers formed their own mental conceptions. In Alexandria, the home of the brilliant philosophic school of Neo-Platonists, to whom Christianity owes so much, there lived one aged teacher, a Libyan of Cyrenaica, whose name was Arius. He held the position of official exponent of Scripture in the Alexandrian Church. In speaking of our Lord, he used the Greek expression ἦν πότε οὐκ ἦν, which being translated means: "There was a time when He was not," implying that in origin, the Infinite Creative Spirit was in being, antecedent to His self-expression in the Logos who was incarnated in Jesus. The bitterest controversy that has ever agitated the Church arose. Eusebius the historian says, "Bishop rose against bishop and district against district, and the Christian world was rent in twain." The Emperor Constantine, at that time ruling the vast Roman Empire, who knew nothing and cared less about the points in dispute, but who disliked dissension in the Empire, summoned the Bishops of the whole Church to a council at Nicæa in Bithynia, and the celebrated "Council of Nice" met under the Presidency of Constantine on June 14, A.D. 325.

There was present at the Council a young deacon whose name was Athanasius. No reports of the prolonged discussion have been preserved, but the brilliant eloquence, profound learning, dauntless courage, and intense conviction of young Athanasius carried all before him, and the result was the condemnation of

Arius, and the production of the Nicene Creed, which is the accepted creed of the whole Christian Church, up to the point where the Creed ended at the Council of Nicæa. The final battle was fought over the insertion of one minute letter in a Greek word, the letter i, or as in Greek, iota. The question was: Was Jesus "Homoousion" "of one substance" with the Father, or was He "Homoiousion," of "similar substance" with the Father? The eloquence of Athanasius was sufficient to cast out the i, the iota, and the words, "Of one substance with the Father," were inserted in the Creed, which was then signed by nearly all the bishops at the Council. Constantine, a professed Christian, who had established Christianity as the State religion of the Empire, had, strangely enough, never been baptized. He was baptized before his death in the Church of St. John Lateran at Rome by a bishop, who, though he signed the Creed at Nicæa, had subsequently relapsed into Arianism.

The latter part of the Creed, beginning with the words, "And I believe in the Holy Ghost," was added forty-four years afterwards at the Council of Constantinople, and the insertion of the words, "proceeding from the Father and the Son," called the "*filioque* clause," originated the schism between the Eastern and the

Western Churches which exists at this day.

Now, though the word "Trinity" does not appear in any formula, except in the production called the "Athanasian Creed," to which the name of Athanasius is fraudulently attached, and though the doctrine is not to be found in its fully developed form in the Scriptures, we, as loyal and convinced Churchmen, accept the language of the Nicene Creed in its entirety. It is an incomparable expression of profound philosophic thinking. The words, "Begotten of His Father before all worlds, being of one substance with the Father," are positively inspired; at the same time no council of the Church can bind our thoughts, and we are justified in using our reason, and asking the question: Does the doctrine of the Trinity approve itself to the rational faculty; does it give us love as well as truth; does it reach down to the scources of our being, and move us to diviner practice in every-day life? In order to answer the question it is necessary to separate the idea underlying the word "Trinity" from the word itself. The word "Trinity" is not in the Bible, it does not occur in the Apostles' Creed, the Lord's Prayer, or the Ten Commandments; it is not therefore obligatory upon the laity at all; nevertheless, as the word does not hamper our privilege to think, and is sanctioned by custom, we need not quarrel with it, so long as it is not used to embitter controversy or to condemn others. Calvin said that he was willing that the word "Trinity" should be forgotten, if only it could be the accepted faith of all, that Father, Son and Holy Spirit, each distinguished by a peculiar property, are one God. "Hear, O Israel," said Jesus, when challenged to declare the basal principle of His religion, "Hear, O Israel, the Lord our God is one Lord." Whatever, therefore, the word Trinity may imply to some minds, it need not mean to us that there are three Gods, neither are we sinning against orthodoxy if we reject the idea of three Persons, in the conventional, colloquial signification of the word "Person." The Latin word *persona* means "a mask," not a "person." Augustine repudiates the word "Person" and accounts for the use of it by the poverty of the Latin language as compared with the Greek. He says the word *Persona* leads to the conception of Father, Son and Spirit as mechanically distinct, instead of livingly inter-penetrating one another. Now you can only reach the root of a dogma by penetrating through all verbal statements to the Eternal Principle underlying it. What is the Eternal Principle underlying the dogma of the Trinity? It is that the Infinite Originating

Mind is one and indivisible; that in His perfect unity there is elementally included a Tri-unity, a Threeness, not of separate individualities, but of essentially separate functionings of the same individuality, by the revelation of which we are assured that absolute power, perfect love, and complete holiness enwrap the human being, in an eternal purpose, in every department of his life. The conception is as old as human thought. The religious history of the human race everywhere witnesses to a realization of threeness of function in the Supreme Intelligence, undefined until revealed in the Christian Faith. It underlies Zoroastrianism, it is enshrined in Hinduism, it is discoverable in the oldest Eastern Scriptures, where it is said of Brahm that " of him thou canst predicate nothing but his threeness." He is " Sat," or Absolute Being; " Kit," Absolute Being thinking itself into duality, expressing itself in the phenomena of the universe and in mankind; " Ananda," Absolute Being in loving, stimulating operation upon the phenomena of the universe and upon the hearts of men. Sat, Kit, Ananda; God in essence, God in manifestation, God in outflowing life; and these three are one. The study of comparative religions prepares for the definite creed which has come to us in its fullness through the

Christian Revelation. The God of Christianity, "in knowledge of Whom standeth our eternal life," has led us to think of Him as, first, the Parent-Source from Whom are all things, for "of Him and through Him and to Him are all things." This is God in essential Being named God the Father. Secondly, inasmuch as the Parent-Source is Infinite, and the human mind "cannot think" Personality of the Infinite, the "Personalness" and moral qualities of the Infinite Parent-Source were for purposes of recognition specialized in one unique human personality, so completely, that Jesus, the embodiment of the Logos, God's thought of Himself, said, "he that hath seen Me hath seen the Father"; and yet He implied that there was so much more in the Parent-Source to be ultimately known that He also said "the Father is greater than I." In other words, the Infinite is greater than His most perfect specialization. This is named God in self-utterance, or God the Son. And, thirdly, the perpetual influence, or spirit, or atmosphere of the Parent-Source as He was manifested in Jesus, ceaselessly operating in our inmost being, suffusing and stimulating our hereditary divine germ, thinking the thought within us, praying the prayer within us, empowering, guiding, sanctifying; and this is named God the Holy Ghost; and these Three are distinct divine functionings of the One Infinite Mind. There is nothing contrary to reason in this conception of the Trinity, and no man honours God by professing belief in that which contradicts his reason. Most of us can probably remember mental perplexity in early youth, when we were almost unconsciously beginning to reason, and were taught, in so many words, that there were three Gods, and yet that there was only one God. If we asked questions, we were told that it was an unintelligible divine mystery which it was sinful to criticize, and that all who rejected it " without doubt would perish everlastingly." So we silently accepted Tritheism until we were old enough to think for ourselves.

But, rational as this conception is, it is necessary to defend it against opponents who quote arithmetic, mechanics and the Council of Nicæa against us. Obviously the starting-point of all philosophic thinking is hypothesis. You cannot prove Infinite Mind antecedent to phenomena, and the self-contemplation of Infinite Mind producing the Logos, and, through the Logos, all the worlds. You cannot prove it; but to the philosophic mind it is an irresistible inference and it contradicts no scientific discovery. Obscurantists might be challenged to explain how " the tree that shelters them comes out of the seed that can be blown from the fingers' ends," and what was the *causa causans* of the first seed, before they make their own limitations the criterion of the verities of the Infinite Mind. But as a matter of fact, so far as scientific criticism is concerned, Physical Science has been constantly demonstrating that threeness of function, in complete unity of essence, is not a theological conundrum, but a recognized fact of the phenomena of nature. I have often quoted Professor Tyndal's demonstrations before the Royal Society, when he showed us that any intensely heated body emits at the same time three rays, wholly differing in their results, but forming such a unity as to be inseparable. There is first the "heat ray," which is felt but not seen; there is secondly, the "light ray," which is seen but not felt; there is, thirdly, the "Actinic ray," which is neither felt nor seen, and which is only known by its chemical action upon certain sensitive substances, such as in the operations of photography. And these three are one; and yet one is not the other, and not one can exist except in conjunction with the other. It is a scientific echo of the self-revelation of the Infinite Mind as adored by the millions of Christendom. The Father, Infinite Mind, felt, as the Soul of the universe, but not seen; "No man hath seen God at any time." The Son, Infinite Mind specialized, the light-ray, "I am the Light of the World," seen but not felt, that is to say not touched except by the touch of Faith, "though the multitudes thronged Him." The Holy Ghost, Infinite Mind in outflowing life, neither seen nor felt, but known by His effects in conversion, renewal, sanctification; helping the heart of man to manifest the immanent God when the Christ in him is stimulated by the "Light of the World" poured into it from the knowledge and teaching of the objective Christ. The analogies of nature, therefore, so far as they go, forbid the thinker to allow that "threeness in unity" is either unphilosophical or absurd. "The meanest flower that blows" can not only "oft-times bring thoughts that lie too deep for tears," but can also present, as in a picture lesson, as veritable a trinity in unity as God Himself. This is my favourite analogy which I repeat every Trinity Sunday. Hold in your hand a full-blown rose; you are holding a perfect model of the rational conception of the Trinity. You are holding first, essential life, that divine mystery which haunts and pervades the minutest microscopic capillaries of the tiniest blade of grass; you are holding, econdly, visible form or manifestation, that evolution of beauty in which essential life has clothed itself, and in which essential life is manifested; and, thirdly, from these two, there comes forth the subtle mystery of perfume pervading your senses; and though essential life is not manifestation, and manifestation is not perfume, these three are essentially and indivisibly one, though their functioning is wholly distinct. Essential life is the Parent Source of the rose; visible form is the manifestation of the rose; and proceeding from parent-source and manifestation is perfume, which is the spirit, or outflowing influence of the rose; and these three are completely distinct in function, and absolutely one in essence.

It would be easy to multiply analogies. A common magnet provides a model of this philosophical conception of the Trinity. To begin with, no one knows what a magnet is, or why it is, what it is. Then first, there is the nature-power that holds atoms together; who can define it? recent science tells you it is the vibration of vortex rings; it is just a fact that defies denial though to account for it you must invent a hypothesis. Secondly, you have the tangible weight that you hold in your hand, visible, objective. Thirdly, you have the out-flowing influence, or magnetism, which draws atoms of steel to itself; what is it? how does it act? the influence is imponderable, invisible, unanalysable, but it is the outflowing power of the two other entities, and these three are one. And just as the trinity of essential life, visible form, and perfume in the rose is all mine so long as I hold fast to the embodiment or manifestation; just as the trinity in the magnet is in my possession while I retain my grasp of the objective tangible weight, so is every attribute of the Holy Trinity mine, so long as I identify myself by faith with the Lord Jesus, the specialization, the Revealer; for "in Him dwelleth all the fulness of the Godhead bodily," and we are complete in Him.

Now briefly observe how the three texts I have quoted illustrate this threeness of function of the Divine Unity. First, Jesus said, "No man cometh unto the Father but by Me." What did He mean?

When you have resisted the tendency theologically to divide God, as it were, against Himself; when you have freed your mind from ingenious subtleties as to one Person in the Trinity satisfying the justice, or buying the mercy of another Person in the Trinity, you see that the Father is Infinite Mind in Essential Being. The Son is Infinite Mind in specialization. The Holy Ghost is Infinite Mind in Outflowing Life. Therefore God is Jesus, and Jesus is the Holy Ghost, and the Holy Ghost is God; and you see that Jesus, the specialization, enables you to think Personality and Fatherhood into your conception of Infinite Mind without losing the sense of His Universality. Without this specialization in Jesus, the power of mentally personalizing the Infinite Mind as our Father would not have been possible. So we come unto the Father through Jesus.

Secondly He said, "No man cometh unto Me except the Father draw him."

How obvious it is that the affinity of man to the all Originating Mind, Immanent in every life-centre that He has thought-formed, is the drawing power, the suggester, of that natural craving for a closer knowledge of the qualities of the Originating Mind whence we came. Now this knowledge can only come in its fulness when the specialization of God in Jesus is recognized. Thus does the Father the Infinite Mind draw His children mentally to seek for, and ultimately to discover, His true nature as it is revealed in Jesus. Thus the Father draws us to Jesus. Then thirdly: "No man can say that Jesus is the Lord but by the Holy Ghost." This saying too is perfectly clear. The Holy Ghost is the "Spirit of Jesus," Jesus functioning from the plane of the Universal, the ceaseless outflowing activity of the Jesus-revelation of the Infinite Mind. The Holy Ghost is the " Christ in you the hope of glory," it is His guiding suggesting moulding power within you that leads you at last to make the " Christ in you " the Lord of your being. And so no man can say that his Jesus-self, the self in him which is in identity with Jesus, his essential self, is now his Lord, ruling his whole being, except by the Holy Ghost.

What is the use of this consideration ? Well, none, absolutely none, if its only object is to defend a metaphysical definition. Religion is not creed but conduct, not orthodoxy but activity. One heterodox lover of humanity is worth a wilderness of orthodox self-seekers. But this festival of the Holy Trinity declares once more the inseverability of God and man, and that God's life in man and around man is the great discovery that brings perfect peace. Love in Origin called God the Father, Love in Action called God the Son, Love in Eternal procession called God the Holy Ghost ensphere your life. There is essentially no possibility of Absence from God. " In Him you live and move and have your being." God surrounds and fills you as the air surrounds you and fills you. The only absence from God is mental, the human mind turned away from God. And this dear God, who longs to realize Himself in His human vehicles, pleads with hearts this day as He has never ceased to plead since we became conscious beings. That whisperer of better things, that convictor of wrong actions, that inspirer of holy desires, that perpetual protestor within us against a mere animalized existence, on this His special festival day, once more says to us as He said on Whit Sunday, "Do you not know that I love you, that I dwell in you, that you are my manifestors, that your bodies are temples of the Holy Ghost?" "Know ye not that the Spirit of God dwelleth in you?" "He that is joined to the Lord is one spirit"; "be ye transformed by the renewing of your minds."

And every up-rising of pure aspiration, every clinging to principle under temptation, every brave acceptance and endurance of the Cross, every choice of abstract right above conventional selfishness, every drowning of animal passion by instant appeal to the Christ within, every preference of a truth that inherits a cross, over a lie that flatters with a promise of ease, is offering to God the Holy Trinity, in fact and in reality, that adoration which we ceaselessly and often thoughtlessly present to

Him with our lips, when we say " Glory be to the Father, and to the Son and to the Holy Ghost: as it was in the beginning is now and ever shall be world without end, Amen."

## SEEING GOD

"Blessed are the pure in heart: for they shall see God."—MATT. v. 8.

INTERESTING questions have come to me, I answer them by reiterating a line of thought which I have made familiar. Can we see God? What is seeing God? Why does our Lord say that only the pure in heart shall see God?

Who are the pure in heart? Conventionality has placed a narrowing limitation upon the words "pure" and "purity" which the Greek word *Catharos*, translated "pure," will not honestly sustain. Of course one meaning of the word is unsoiled, implying that spiritual perception is dependent on moral life, and that a mind wilfully filled with carnal imaginings and sensual desires, and purposely retaining them, will find it psychologically impossible to attain to the higher God-consciousness which is "seeing God." Where the mind is perpetually functioning towards the gratification of the senses, and not towards the internal Kingdom of heaven, which is above the senses, a film grows over the spiritual eyesight, and then the very potentiality, which would not be but for man's divine origin, is perverted, it becomes a negation of God instead of an expression of God, producing horrors which do not exist in the animal world, which are only possible in the human world; horrors like those exposed in Miss Elizabeth Robins' new book, in connexion with what is called "the White Slave traffic." This is the devil, and the only devil, and full devil enough without the traditional anti-god with the cloven foot. Such hearts of course do not see God, they only see the devil within them, and that is the negation and perversion of their divine nature.

But the full meaning of the word *Catharos*, translated pure, though including physical and mental chastity, is far wider. *Catharos* means clear, open, free, unlimited.

"*En Catharo*" means "in an open space"; the word is classically used for a tract of land that has been cleared of trees. So, freed from limitation, the Beatitude is. Blessed are they whose mental horizon has been so enlarged by clearing away the trees of traditional wrong thinking, that, while rightly based on the dogmatic theology of the Church as their starting point for thought, they recognize the limitless Infinity of the Cosmic consciousness, and the Universal Immanence of the Creative Spirit. Blessed are they, for they, and they only, shall see God as He really is. With them the action of the understanding, and the yearnings of the heart, have combined to open their eyes to perceive an Infinite mind, which, while it includes the senses, is above, beyond, and around the senses, and they know that "God is all and all is God."

Immeasurable is the peace of thus seeing the love-presence of God, the Infinite Spirit, in all His manifestations; of recognizing the Soul of souls, the Father-Spirit as the inmost element of all elements.

The longing to see God is instinctive, it is the stirring of heredity, but it is well not to confuse "seeing God" with our experience of seeing with human eyes an objective form. When Augustine cried "O my God, let me see Thee, and if to see Thee is to die, let me die that I may see Thee," he was still under the dominion of that limited conception. The answer of the Originating Spirit is ever the same, whether given to Moses, to the disciples of Jesus, to Augustine, or to you and me, "No man can see my face and live." It is the clear statement that no living being can see the face or form of God, as a separate personal face or form, because God has not got a separate face or form. It also means that while man lives under earth conditions he cannot fully realize the universal individuality of the Infinite Spirit as he will be able to realize it when he has his new senses in the other sphere of being. The conditions which would make this possible would make earth life and education impossible. It would imply the "Nirvana" of the perfect, which will be conscious identification with universal life without the loss of your own sense of individuality, which, in earth conditions, has only been vouchsafed to one human being. The silver cord of limitations must be loosed, and the golden bowl of atomic enclosure must be broken, before man can really see God. And then, "seeing God" will not be looking upon a Person but an intense thrilling consciousness that all is God.

Others before Augustine have asked to see God. Moses, for example, said "Show me Thy Glory." Isaiah complained almost petulantly "Thou hidest Thyself, O God of Israel." The Disciples of Jesus asked to see God. The answer is always the same. You can only see God in His manifestations. Remember the answer given to Moses, "Thou canst not see my face, but I will make my goodness pass before thee." In other words "I will manifest my qualities in phenomena." And as the spiritual intuition follows that clue, reason, and the recognition of beauty, and logic reveal the Originating Spirit, and St. Paul's words become true, "That which may be known of God is manifest, for the invisible things of Him are clearly seen through the things that are made." And, following this clue, we can arrive, as the highest mystics did arrive, at the consciousness that we live and move in a divine Presence, which Divine Presence is the Originator and the Substance of all that is, so that by degrees we become intuitively certain that an Omnipotent, Invisible Father-Mother-Soul is always with us, only awaiting our recognition and receptivity.

The human mind has always been impatient of this law of the Originating Spirit, and the result has been narrowness, superstition, sacerdotalism which have clouded spiritual eyesight. Conformists to the inherited representations of religion, in every age, have satisfied the desire for a visible God with idols, or with doctrinal limitations which are idols of the mind, and have execrated and persecuted when they could, all winged souls who had mentally outgrown their limitations and defective

Theism. He who recognizes the logical necessity of an immaterial creative mind building up a material universe from its own thought-substance is " seeing God." God makes " His goodness pass before him " ; he sees God in the beauty, harmony, invariableness of the natural order of the Cosmos. He reads God's name in the lovely sweep of the frost flowers on his window-pane, in the glittering jewels which encrust every spray and twig when the rime clings to the branches ; he sees that everything must have come from the imagination of an Infinite Originating Mind. He sees that the whole creation is, because it expresses a central life, he sees that God who "sleeps in the stone dreams in the plant, wakens in the animal and is self-conscious in the human animal." He thinks into the facts of conscience, personality, will, love, self-sacrifice, he asks himself whence they come, and follows them logically to their origin ; his inward vision clears, he begins to see that he himself is a product of the Divine Mind imaging forth an image of Itself, and, agreeing with Descartes that there must be in the Originating Cause as much as in the sum total of all its effects, he begins to " see God," that is he is entering into God-consciousness. He sees physical beauty in the universe, and moral beauty in man ; Logic convinces him that there must be a Divine creative ideal of both physical and moral beauty, and that this Divine creative ideal can only be an Infinite Originating Mind; and a heart that has arrived at this attitude finds its thoughts transfigured, its aspirations invigorated, because it is rescued from limitations, it is becoming *Catharos,* pure, "an open space," and instead of looking for God as an isolated personality, such an one sees God everywhere, and his highest longing is to realize more the Being and the Presence of the Infinite and Eternal Spirit-Mind from which all things proceed.

How did our Lord answer His disciples when they asked that they might see God? He implied that they would only see Him through His manifestations. He had encouraged their desire for God. He had intensified their soul-thirst, until at last, one of them, as the spokesman of the rest, bursts out with the old cry based upon the old error, "Lord show us the Father, and it sufficeth us." The answer is always the same; to Moses it is: "I will make My goodness pass before thee"; to Philip it is: "You will never see the Father as a person here, or elsewhere, you will know Him in His manifestations. I am His highest manifestation, the specialized embodiment of His qualities, the express image of His Being.

Have I been so long time with you, and yet hast thou not known me, Philip? He that hath seen Me hath seen the Father."

There is no other answer. "Seeing God," a thrilling recognition of the Presence of God, becomes possible to those whose mental horizon has been so enlarged by right thinking that they have recognized that the life of God is within all, and they will find God within themselves. Jesus said "The Kingdom of God is within you," it is this essential nearness of God, this elemental truth of the oneness of man with the Infinite Spirit, that causes God not to be discoverable by the senses.

> "The lark flew up in the morning bright,
> And sung and balanced on sunny wings;
> And this was its song: 'I see the light;
> I look on a world of beautiful things,
> But flying and singing everywhere,
> In vain have I searched to find the air.'"

And God is in us, and we in God, in a far higher, more transcendent sense than the bird is in the air and the air in the bird, and the "pure in heart," the minds enlarged from limitations, see it and rejoice.

Personally I am always far more able to see God in others than in myself, though it is well to know your own divinity, and appeal to it. The immanent divine in every lovable character mirrors forth and distributes the qualities of the Parent-Spirit. Did you ever love a human being so intensely that to you that one was a manifestation of God, so complete, that you wanted nothing more? There was no disloyalty to Infinite Spirit in that, on the contrary, God was making His "goodness pass before you" in that life, and wherever down the ages, man has shown courage, self-sacrifice, love, he has, ipso facto, made God's goodness pass before men, "and shown the Father." This "urge," this pressure of the divine in man, often manifests when the manifestor does not know that it is "God working in him." God is "self-conscious in man" when man does not know it. Twelve years ago David Rutter was released after twenty-seven years' penal servitude. He had kept silence for twenty-seven years knowing he was innocent; he had borne the blame of a great crime for another man. The man who had committed the crime had a young wife and young children. Rutter was alone in the world, and, for the sake of his friend, took the whole guilt on himself. Was not God "self-conscious" in David Rutter? Didn't he "make God's goodness pass before men"?

"God wakens in the animal." In a recent newspaper was an account of a captain swept from his ship in one of the recent storms, and saved by his brown setter dog who leapt after him and held him up till the lifeboat rescued him. Didn't God " waken " in that brown setter?

This Universal principle, this seeing God in His manifestations, was supremely exhibited in the Lord Jesus, the One Perfect Individual Life-centre. Infinite Spirit " made His goodness pass before us " in that Unique Specimen of the race. In Him God so perfectly realized Himself, and expressed Himself, that when the demand, " Show us the Father," was made to Jesus He was able to reply: " I am the specialization of the qualities of God. He that hath seen Me hath seen the Father."

This is the meaning of the Epiphany. The story of the star leading thoughtful Zoroastrians across the wilderness to Bethlehem, is the analogy of the secret drawing of the Infinite Mother-Heart, appealing to the deepest instincts of the human conscience, sometimes obscured for a season, but leading on, through " the altar stairs of things created, that slope through darkness up to God," suggesting the immanence of an Infinite Soul, stimulating the longing for a keener knowledge of that Infinite Soul; leading on, till at last it " comes and stands over where the young Child is," the one perfect manifestation of God in the man Christ Jesus, and the heart, the pure heart, the unclouded heart cries out : " I see, humanity is the Incarnation, humanity is the manifestation of God, and the one perfect specimen of humanity is the full-orbed vision of God, and in Jesus I see God."

If this Epiphany lesson were learnt the world would be redeemed. The immanence of God is the monopoly of no age, no nation, no Church, no religion. To the " pure in heart who see God " there are no barriers, separating nation from nation, man from man, religion from religion. If men thus saw God, they would know that behind all expressions of the hereditary God-necessity there is only one religion, and one God, and the hostilities of rival Churches, and the senseless suspicions of rival nations would pass away. God's life in man is the one basal principle of unity. When it is realized, and not before in spite of all Hague conventions, will come the time :

> " When the war drum throbs no longer
> And the battle flag is furled
> In the Parliament of man
> The Federation of the world."

Now all this is not an opinion to hold, or a creed to follow, it is a life to live. We see the truth in the universal as God's ideal, it is for us, as individuals, to apply it in the particular.

The question to ask is, What does it mean to me? Well, one thing is certain; nothing, positively nothing, will so lift you above the worries and vexations of transient time as an intense conviction of the constant nearness of Infinite Divine Love, and the inseverability of God and man. Then, again, whatever convinces you that you are yourself a reflection, an image, of Infinite Spirit; that within you, and within your loved ones wherever they be, abides a Divine life than can never die, and never become disintegrated, which Divine life seeks recognition, and desires manifestation, must affect, with surpassing power, the practice of your life, and the peace of your soul. It stimulates you to live after the Spirit, it liberates you from carnal desires and the dominion of the senses, it leads you to see in every trial, in the bitterness of bereavement, in the discipline of physical pain and bodily weakness, the working of the Father's promise of a nobler manhood earned by courageous endurance of tribulation. God has identified Himself with you; in a sense, God is you. He will meet your difficulties, and face your worries, and help you to bear your pains, because He is "the Power that worketh in you."

This supreme assurance intensely emphasises our responsibility as vehicles, manifestors, of

God. If we have the knowledge which comes from the pure, the emancipated heart, the duty of "making God's goodness pass before men" becomes very real and urgent. That is why God made you, it is what God wants you for. God cannot do without you. Indeed, a God who could do without you would be a God whom you could do without, and you and God would be on separate planes, instead of being, as you are, essentially one.

When we know that God is Infinite Spirit expressed in phenomena, and that He has thought-generated human beings as living vehicles through whom He desires to function, that He means us to be distributing centres of His life, His qualities, His love, we have made a discovery which alters our whole view of life, and suggests a relation to God of vast responsibility. Far more complete with us should be the control of the senses, the peace and joy of trust in the experience of pain, sorrow, and trial, the manifestation of love to unlovable people. This is our knowledge, are we living it ? Would the Christ be justified in saying to us, as He said to the orthodox members of the Church of His nation : You think yourselves a chosen people, I tell you many shall come from the east and from the west, contemplative Buddhists ; self-denying Brahmins, spiritually-minded people whom you call heretics; men and women who lived their lives fully up to the light they had, and so made the world the better that they had lived; they shall " sit down in the kingdom," that is, they shall find themselves in a high spiritual sphere, when many of the children of the kingdom, for all their orthodox creeds, correct ceremonial, and intellectual knowledge, will be " cast out," that is, sent back to school in one of our Father's many training spheres, that they may attain God consciousness.

This is, then, the thought for to-day. To be " pure in heart " is not only to be morally clean, but also to see only one Power in the Universe and in your life. " To see God " is to see the life of God Epiphanized everywhere, and transcendently manifested in the Perfect Divine Man. We are, above all, to attain to the knowledge of God's indwelling Presence in ourselves, which is only awaiting recognition to be our abundant supply.

As the soul is opened inwardly to the Immanence of the Infinite, the eye of the spirit will see Him more and more clearly. We know that it is so here. We see Him to-day more clearly than we did a year ago, and we are confident that the future has inconceivable surprises in store for us which it cannot now enter into the mind of man to conceive.

In the meanwhile the individuality of each one of us is a functioning centre of the Infinite Mind, and He desires to realize Himself, and express Himself, in and through our mortal bodies.

It is well never to leave our room in the morning without having earnestly petitioned :—

" Our Father, I pray that I may live this day in constant recollection of my true relation, as an individual, to Thee, the Originating and Indwelling Spirit. May my conscious mind perceive that Thy Life, Thy Spirit, Thy Thoughts are within me, and that Thou art seeking to realize Thyself, and to manifest Thy Love through me."

To live, one day at a time, in this attitude of mind, is gradually to see God more and more clearly, and to go to rest each night with the peaceful affirmation :—

" One sweetly solemn thought comes to me more and more,
I am nearer home to-day than I have ever been before."

# PETER

"But when Peter was come to Antioch, I withstood him to the face, because he was to be blamed."
—GAL. ii. 11.

A MEMORABLE scene indeed. Paul, "the little one," as his name implies, whose "bodily presence" was, according to his own testimony, "contemptible," but whose spirit was on fire with enthusiasm, standing up to the infallible Pontiff and laughing his infallibility to scorn. This apostolic fracas, which we can visualize in our imagination, is to me intensely suggestive. We are living in interesting times. In spite of the immense place which the material universe holds in the thoughts of men, and the great advance in practical science, there has arisen in this twentieth century a keen interest in the spiritual world. It is as though the first raindrops of the refreshment promised in the words, "I will pour out My spirit upon all flesh," were falling upon thirsty souls. There is a marked synthesis of thought upon the transcendent truth of the thrilling nearness of God as universally diffused individuality self-expressed in phenomena. This is not Pantheism. This does not sublimate away the idea of God into a vague essence, for the Christian philosophy teaches that the God Who "sleeps in the stone, dreams in the plant, wakens in the animal, and is self-conscious in man," has been specialized, so completely, in Jesus Christ, that in Him we are able to think personality of the Infinite Mind, while at the same time preserving our sense of its universality. Thus a right understanding of the Incarnation saves believers in universal Immanence from the vagueness of Pantheism. Now, considering the extraordinary variety of the religious imagination, it is not surprising that one result of this newly awakened spiritual sense should be the uprising of a perfect swarm of societies, associations, new thought circles, higher thought centres, and so on, tending to perplexity, disruption, and alienation from the visible Church. To join them is, in my opinion, a mistake. All of these multitudinous amalgams possess some portion of truth, all are evidence of the Divine breath, all are indications of the new hunger for spiritual knowledge, while not one of them possesses a monopoly of God's truth. What should be our attitude towards them? My advice is, assimilate gratefully what each can contribute, and remain where you are in the Church of your Baptism. Go forth, mentally, and receptively, and feed upon their literature and their teaching, as the bee goes forth from her hive into a garden of flowers, gathering honey from this bloom and from that bloom, and returning to her hive where is her home and her store. Personally, I have gained some spiritual honey from every one of them, from Abdul Baha to Christian Science, and I come back to the hive of the Catholic Church with a sense of rest, and a renewed satisfaction and appreciation, bringing with me some spiritual honey from every flower I have mentally explored. While it is impossible not to gain honey from the earnest, upward thinking of these seeking souls, one also meets with philosophical theories which are wholly erroneous, and, almost invariably, with a total misunderstanding of the unique position of our Blessed Lord, as the one perfect specialization of the Logos, and, in that sense, "the only Son of God," and one comes back to the Apostles' Creed, and notably to that masterpiece of philosophic thought, the Nicene Creed, with a sigh of thankfulness. "I believe in the Holy Catholic Church," the visible Church, the Church founded by Christ and taught by Him during the forty days, and based upon the Apostles' doctrine and fellowship. I believe that Infinite Immanent Mind has given us in the visible Church a means of grace, a means of realizing and appropriating His personal contact with the human life-centres in which He has expressed Himself. I believe in the virtue of ordination, and I believe that spiritual energy of a subtle kind is brought into direct relation with the souls of men by the sacraments of the Church duly administered, and believingly received. But, why do I say this, and what has the contest between Paul and Peter to do with the question? Just this. That it proves to me conclusively that my hive, my branch of the Holy Catholic Church, which is my spiritual home, wherein is my store of honey, cannot lawfully be dominated, coerced, by any other branch of the Church Universal assuming supremacy and authority over it. I loathe controversy, but on St. Peter's Day, one is drawn to inspect the Rock from whence we are hewn, and sweep some of the dust from its surface. Is Peter the Rock, or is Christ? The assertion of Papal supremacy over all other Christian Churches is virtually based upon the words of this morning's Gospel, reported to have been spoken by Our Lord to Peter: "Blessed art thou, Simon Bar-jona: for flesh and blood hath not revealed it unto thee, but My Father which is in heaven. And I say unto thee, That thou art Peter, and upon this rock I will build My Church, and I will give unto thee the keys of the kingdom of heaven, and whatsoever thou shalt bind on earth shall be bound in heaven, and whatsoever thou shalt loose on earth shall be loosed in heaven." Now whether this is one of the passages in the New Testament "improved" in the direction of orthodoxy by the *correctores*, appointed for the purpose after the Council of Nicæa, I do not know, but one thing I do know, namely, that it is absolutely certain that Paul did not understand the words in the sense attributed to them by the Roman hierarchy, or he could not possibly have been guilty of so grave an act of disloyalty as to withstand to his face an infallible Pontiff "because he was to be blamed."

Now we Anglicans, believing in "differences of administration but the same Lord," can have no quarrel with the Church of Rome as a religion; on the contrary, as a providential adaptation of Christianity to a certain widespread habit of intellectual apprehension it is of great value, and entitled to much more than toleration. Considered as a political system, seeking to attain control over the liberties of Englishmen, our estimate is different, but in this aspect we can leave it to the advancing political intelligence of the democracy of this age of extended suffrage and increasing education. But as a religion, as one of the organized manifestations of the relation between God and the souls of men, the Roman Church builds up many saints, and leads thousands of God's children into the kingdom of heaven. What we are concerned with is the monstrous fiction that Peter was the first infallible Pontiff, and that the Roman Church is the Mother and Mistress of all other Churches, with the power of excommunication over them, a fiction originating from taking the words in this morning's Gospel on the literal plane, and buttressing them by certain documents, known to be forged, called the Isidorian Decretals. Now it is significant—

(1) That any supremacy supposed to be conferred upon St. Peter by these words was wholly ignored by the Apostles themselves, as it was after this incident that we find them engaged in controversy as to who should be the greatest.

(2) That in the first Œcumenical Council, the Council of Jerusalem, James, and not Peter, presided, and Peter was called upon by James to address the Council.

(3) That there is not the faintest evidence in history that Peter ever set his foot in Rome, and it is absolutely certain that there was no bishop in Rome when Paul wrote his Epistle to the Romans, as it is inconceivable that Paul could have wholly ignored the Bishop of Rome, and could have spoken of coming himself to build them up.

(4) That it is as certain, as any fact in history can be said to be certain, that the British Church is older than the Roman Church. Britain was converted during the lifetime of Paul, and at the Council of Arles, in 314, the Bishops of York, London and Lincoln were present, and when Gregory sent a mission to Britain in 596, believing it to be heathen, the missionaries found a Catholic Church with bishops, priests and deacons, in the fastnesses of Wales, whither they had been driven by the invading barbarians.

(5) That precisely the same words as to binding and loosing were spoken by Our Lord to the whole body of the disciples, including the women, when they were assembled in the Upper Chamber after His Resurrection.

(6) The Council of Nicæa laid it down as an irrevocable law that the great sees of Alexandria, Rome and Antioch should be wholly independent of each other, and that there should be no Universal Pontiff. And yet, in defiance of the Council of Nicæa, and of all history, Pope Leo XIII deliberately promulgated a Bull denying the validity of Anglican Orders, and pronouncing all our Sacraments to be a mockery, thus attempting to destroy the Catholicity of the Anglican Communion.

Of course, the Pope's Bull is a matter of profound indifference, and its gross ignorance of history covers his assumption of infallibility with ridicule. The Bull of Leo XIII is, to instructed and intelligent minds, the abolition of the infallibility of the Pope. But this impudent document did service to the Anglican Church. For—

(1) It silenced those who accuse believers in the reality of Sacraments, and in the validity of ordination, absolution, and benediction, of being Romanists in disguise. Whatever we are, we are not Romanists in disguise, for the Pope repudiates us. He calls us a tumultuous mob. The supposed connection be-

tween High Anglicanism and Romanism is severed for ever by the Bull of Leo XIII.

(2) The Pope provided us with one cogent additional proof that the only element in the Church of England that he dreads, as a bulwark against Rome, is that which is called the High Church element. Protestantism, as a negation, no cultivated Roman Catholic fears; but the strong assertion that the Church of England is all, aye and more than all, that the Church of Rome claims to be; that it is a living limb of the Catholic Church, with an unbroken descent from the Apostles—this represents a danger that the Romanist dreads, and against this will the Vatican fulminate its Bulls. The most influential Protestantism, the truest safeguard against Rome, is the strong affirmation of the absolutely equal and independent Catholicity and Apostolicity of the Church of England.

(3) It drew from our Archbishops a really remarkable historical document, vindicating the Anglican position, which was published in *The Times* in 1897. This document has placed the validity

of Anglican orders upon an absolutely irrefragable foundation.

But, enough of this. After all, what does it all matter when once we have found our right relation to Infinite Mind, and have mentally recognized our Identity with the Lord Jesus as the perfect Manifestation of a sonship, a principle, not peculiar to Him, but universal, and therefore ours. We cannot be one penny the worse if the occupant of the Vatican curses us night and day. But we must not leave our thought of Peter at that point on his festival day. He is not responsible for the monstrous fictions built upon his name. In dismissing the fictions we shall have to lose some cherished legends. For example, if Peter never was in Rome, what becomes of the "Domine quo vadis?" And that charming legend of Peter, as the symbol of the Church Universal, bearing up a steep mountain the sins and shortcomings of the Church and fainting under the burden? The legend tells how he met a little child, who said to him: "Place thy burden upon me; now carry me," and as he lifts the child, the burden becomes as a feather. Thus it is with all who have found the Christ within. As the Son-of-God-nature is recognized it will bear every burden of fear and trouble. Well, the legends may go, but what remains is this: We may learn much from Peter. He was lovable, impulsive, and essentially human. He had his faults, he was timid in a crisis; we can well understand that he could never, for the rest of his life, hear a cock crow without a pang of remorse. He was not naturally truthful. Paul, who evidently did not like him, says that "Barnabas was carried away by his dissimulation." But he loved, and love covers a multitude of sins. "Thou knowest all things," he said to Jesus, "Thou knowest that I love Thee." The examination of that love by Our Lord, when He three times asked Peter, "Lovest thou Me?" proves that the condition precedent for the Ministry of the Christ is Love. It is also the condition precedent of the reception of the new spiritual sense. It was that quality of love which gained for Peter the inner illumination which drew from Our Lord the commendation, "Blessed art thou, flesh and blood hath not revealed this to thee, but My Father which is in heaven"; and this is the main lesson of to-day's festival. Peter was the recipient of words from the lips of Our Lord which should be interpreted, not upon the literal and surface plane, but from the mystical standpoint, and universalized. They are meant for each one of us. Consider the words as spoken to yourself. Have you begun to realize that true life is conscious identification with Infinite Life? Have you found the Christ as the specialization of the Divine Principle which is in you? As the witness that Humanity is the son of the living God? Then strike out the name of Simon Bar-jona and insert your own name. The Christ says to you: "Blessed are you, flesh and blood has not revealed this to you." Intellect may do much, it may be most valuable in drawing inferences that are evidential, but it cannot open the eyes of the soul. The eyes of your soul are open, God within you has opened them. Now that your eyes are opened you are one of the stones, the foundation stones, on which the Kingdom of Heaven is being built in men's hearts. "I will give unto you the keys" of your own Kingdom of Heaven. "The Kingdom of Heaven is within you," and the key to that kingdom is the new spiritual sense which unlocks the knowledge, hidden from the natural reason, that you are a Temple of the Holy Ghost, a shrine of the Universal Christ, a vehicle and distributor of the Indwelling Spirit. With that knowledge, with that key, you are the arbiter of your own destiny, the judge and purifier of your own self, and what you bind on earth is bound in heaven. In other words, the only absolution for an illuminated soul is self-absolution. You are never unforgiven by Infinite Mind, but it is you, your higher self, the Christ in you, " the great white throne " of judgment within you, that judges you. Our Lord said: " I came not to judge the world, man hath One that judgeth him, the Word (the realized Logos, his own ideal humanity) that shall judge him." What is the conclusion? Keep yourself in a receptive attitude towards the luminous love-Presence in you and around you. Establish by assiduous mental practice a confidence between yourself and the indwelling spirit till it becomes the normal attitude of your life. There will then be no future " fearful looking for of judgment." What you loose on earth, the evil within you from which you become emancipated on earth, will be loosed in heaven. The indwelling divinity, which flesh and blood knew not, but which has been revealed to you by the Father in the heaven within you, will be to you a perpetual Judge and a guiding mind, and you will realize more and more that you are an expression of the Infinite Spirit. Then you will be increasingly able to meet every discipline with the affirmation: " Love, Wisdom, and Truth are working within me, God is all, and all is God, and God is Love." Then you will have found the secret of peace, and the antidote to worry, and the road to patience, for it is promised—

> "Thou shalt keep him in perfect peace
> Whose mind is stayed on Thee."

# GRIEVING THE SPIRIT

" Grieve not the Holy Spirit."—EPH. iv. 30.

THE thesis laid down in the previous sermon was that we are never unforgiven by Infinite Mind, and that the only absolution an awakened soul needs is self-absolution. Paul says in Ephesians iv., " Grieve not the Holy Spirit " ; in other words, you cannot make God angry, but you can cause Him grief.

Our Lord said, " God is Spirit " (not " a " Spirit, there is no article in the Greek). St. John said, " God is love." Therefore, Spirit is Love and Love is Spirit, and Paul says, " Grieve not the Spirit." He does not say, " beware of the wrath, the indignation of the Spirit." He implies that the only emotion that wrong-doing can excite in Infinite Love is grief, and the Spirit is Infinite Love. We know we cannot define Spirit. Webster says, "Spirit is intelligence apart from embodiment." Spinoza says, " Spirit is Infinite and Eternal substance." Spirit is the Infinite Creative Mind which has brought all visible things into existence. Spirit has produced the millions of glittering worlds, by mentally concentrating the particles of the universal primary ether into cosmic form. Spirit, therefore, is Infinite. It is the All, and as God is Spirit, God is All and All is God. We cannot mentally grasp the conception, but it is lovely to think into it and lose yourself in it. You can lose yourself by thinking into the stupendous immensity of the visible universe. Our sun, alone, is 330,000 times as large as our earth, and then remember this limitless universe is a visible expression of Spirit, and the constraining motive power of the Originating Spirit is Love. And Spirit loves the vehicles in which It has expressed Itself with an intensity proportioned to the degree and dignity of Its self-realization, from the grass, the lily, and the bird, to man; and the supreme culminating point of the love of Spirit for Its manifestations is Man. The problem of life, then, as I have often said, consists in finding the true relation of the Individual to the Originating Spirit. Mr. Troward has called the creative act "the self-contemplation of Infinite Mind." This is a modern way of expressing Plato's doctrine of the Logos, which was adopted by Philo, and assimilated by Greek Christian theology. The Logos is God's thought of Himself, and when He thinks that thought it becomes differentiated, by an orderly sequence of evolution, into the phenomena of the universe, and these phenomena all express some of the qualities of which the Infinite Mind is conscious in Itself. The solar system declares the glory of God, the vegetable world and the animal world express the life and beauty of God, and, after self-realization in mechanical phenomena, Spirit proceeds to a higher self-realization, and images forth an image of Itself into separate individual human life-centres, and man takes his place in the cosmic order. That is how, and why, you and I came into the world; and each of us belongs, in his deepest being, in his individuality, to the creative Spirit. Our real self, our true ego, imaged forth from the Originating Mind, is not the body, and knows no home but the Infinite Spirit of which it is a part, and from which, " trailing clouds of glory, it has come." From these premises two conclusions are obvious—

(1) Universalism.

"That we, and all men move
Under a canopy of Love
As broad as the blue sky above,

> That we on divers shores now cast
> Shall meet, our perilous voyage past,
> All in our Father's home at last."

And (2) our relation to Infinite Spirit is that of voluntary vehicles for His self-manifestation, as contrasted with the automatic vehicles, such as the solar system, and the lily, and the bird. We have the power, not given to the solar system, the lily, and the bird, of grieving the Spirit, disappointing the Spirit, thwarting the Spirit, by using our volition in self-gratification, or in allowing ourselves to worry. Nothing grieves the Spirit more than worrying, and in refusing to allow the Spirit to realize Itself in our own individual lives.

Then I am justified in saying the " Key of the Kingdom of Heaven " within you is the awakened sense which unlocks for you the knowledge, hidden from the natural reason, that you are a Temple of the Spirit, a Shrine of the Logos, a vehicle and distributor of the indwelling Mind. With that knowledge, with that key, you are the arbiter of your own destiny, and the judge and corrector of your own self, and what you " loose " on earth in your self-training is " loosed in heaven." In other words, the only absolution for an illuminated soul is self-absolution. You are never unforgiven by Infinite Mind, but your higher self, the throne of judgment within you, binds you or looses you. That is what Our Lord meant when He said, " I came not to judge the world, man hath one that judgeth him, the Word (that is the Logos within him, his own ideal humanity), that shall judge him." Now I allow that on the plane of traditional rudimentary theology there are many phrases, both in Scripture and in the Liturgy, which seem to bear the meaning that forgiveness of sin is as though an Objective World-Ruler had received some affront which He was content to overlook. There is nothing unsound in this rudimentary conception, it is the logical conclusion from the Measure of Knowledge which the average mind is able to assimilate. But I am not speaking here to the average mind. I am speaking to awakened spiritual consciousnesses, to those to whom it has been said " blessed art thou, flesh and blood has not revealed this to thee, thou didst not arrive at this knowledge through the intellect. The Father, in the heaven within thee, hath taught thee this." It is perfectly natural that at the first feeling of remorse for wrong-doing, we should cry out, " God forgive me," " God be merciful to me, a sinner," but awakened spiritual consciousness will convince you that there can never be the slightest sense of affront on the part of an external God, such as there is when we humans wrong one another. "He that sinneth against me," saith God, "wrongeth his own Soul." He does, because he grieves the Spirit within himself. We know that Infinite Mind is never angry or unforgiving with those that oppose His Love, because He showed us Himself in the Lord Jesus. The Lord Jesus was the heart of Infinite Mind personified for purposes of recognition, and the Lord Jesus said, "If ye only love them that love you, what thank have ye; love your enemies, bless them that curse you." That, then, is the attitude of Infinite Mind, and that is why I say we are never unforgiven by Infinite Mind. Why, you ask, is this not more clearly stated in the New Testament? Well, could it be more clearly stated for those who really believe that Jesus Christ is God, Infinite Mind specialized? Our Lord rarely, if ever, weakened the hold of men's minds upon their rudimentary conceptions, but always under the surface of His utterances there lay the suggestion of the higher truth. You remember when the Pharisees found fault with Him for saying to a paralysed man, "thy sins are forgiven thee"? They took His words literally, on the surface plane, and considered that He had spoken an absolution. On the esoteric plane He had not pronounced an absolution, He had expressed a universal fact. Esoterically His words would mean, " So far as Infinite Mind is concerned you are forgiven, because you have never been unforgiven." He then goes on to say, in language luminous with hidden meaning, " Whether is easier to say, Thy sins are forgiven thee, or to say, Arise, and walk ? " The inner meaning, of course, is that the process of healing sickness, and of forgiveness of sin, is practically identical. Disease is the result of minute organisms preying on the vital tissues; its remedy is the encouragement, within the patient, either by medicine, or massage, or suggestion, of the *vis medicatrix*, the rebuilding power, of the sub-conscious system of the patient himself, which imparts a healthier condition, destroying the hostile bacilli. Disease is forgiven by being cured, and in no other way, and the patient himself cures himself, " binds or looses " his own illness. In the Salpetrière in Paris many cures are effected by suggestion under the hypnotic process, a process which I think open to many objections.

The practitioner suggests healing to the hypnotized patient, the subconscious mind accepts the suggestion, and the patient heals himself. In like manner sin is the result of carnal influences yielded to which lower spiritual vitality, and grieve the Spirit which is seeking to realize Itself, and lust and temper and selfishness are the result. Absolution cannot come by an external world-ruler ceasing to be affronted, but only by the uprising of a purer, healthier life, the life suggested by the Divine Spirit within, the real "I," the true ego, which, when recognized and not grieved, will control and regulate the animal influence. Paul says, "I keep under my body." And when a man can say that, he has realized the Spirit within him and has "loosed" his higher self, and what he has thus loosed on earth is loosed in heaven. What the physician of the body does is to help a man to cure himself, and the healing agency of medicine lies mostly in the fact that it appeals to a fixed belief in its curative power, and so invigorates the *vis medicatrix* in the patient. Similarly the physician of the soul can only really help another by showing him how to help himself; and impressing on his mind that the power is within himself. Neither healing nor forgiveness can be poured into a man from outside; the power is within him. With this esoteric interpretation held in the mind, we can cordially accept the exclamation of the Pharisees, "Who can forgive sins but God only." It is absolutely true, but not in the sense that they meant it, namely that an extra-cosmic objective Deity would overlook transgression, but in the sense that the divine in the man, God immanent, the true spiritual self of the man, has ceased to be grieved, has enabled him to put away his sin and forgive himself, for no man can forgive himself except as he is enabled, through the power of God within him, to put away the sin.

So forgiveness of sins, or in other words, control of the animal nature, is the result of your own use of "the Keys of the Kingdom of Heaven" within you, and those keys are spiritual consciousness and loyalty to it when awakened. Our Lord was sinless, not because He was not tempted, but because He always held those Keys. He lived in spiritual apprehension, and not in the carnal mind. Spiritual apprehension was the actual working consciousness of His life. You remember He said, "the Prince of this world cometh and hath nothing in Me"; the Greek word ἄρχων, translated "Prince," classically means the principle underlying certain lines of action. It is as if our Lord had said the principle that underlies material things, the instinct of animalism, the dominion of the senses, the impulse to retaliation, the fear engendered by mortal conditions, "cometh," but its suggestions are powerless, for in Me it finds nothing to correspond with it, no predisposition, no receptive nidus, no mental home. Just as the principle of infectious diseases to which many are exposed, "cometh," and where it finds no receptive nidus, no predisposition, it cannot propagate, it "hath nothing in them," and they are not harmed. Though the Lord Jesus "suffered being tempted," there was no receptive nidus in Him, though He was of the same flesh and blood as ourselves, because from the first He held "the Keys of the Kingdom of Heaven" within Him. He knew that God was in Him. His basis was "I and the Father are one." At any moment He could mentally withdraw from external conditions into "the secret place of the Most High." He was kept sinless and in perfect peace, because His mind, His conscious mind, His thinking capacity, was absolutely one with the Father-Spirit, Whose unique manifestation He was. Now obviously we cannot say so positively that the dominion of the senses hath nothing in us, but the spirit is in us also. John says, "As He is, so are we in this world," meaning that man, being a spirit, is one with the Universal Spirit. Therefore surely we too (at an infinite distance) can likewise defy "the Prince of this world" by the same process. What is the process? Paul tells us over and over again that the process of using the Keys of your own

Kingdom of Heaven within is mental. "Be ye transformed," he says, "by the renewing of your mind." Again he says, "Be renewed in the spirit of your mind." And again, "Ye have the mind of Christ"; that is, God has given you "the Keys," if you would only know it. "Let this mind be in you which was also in Christ Jesus"; that is, learn to use those keys. In other words, use your will to change the nature of your habitual thinking. The will is the centralizing principle of the conscious mind. The function of the will is to keep the conscious mind stayed on the divinity within you to the exclusion of other thoughts. If "the Prince of this world," in the shape of a carnal, an angry, an unforgiving thought, "cometh," force your mind into a thrilling consciousness of oneness with God. Get into the habit of it, and you will become what you habitually think. If by assiduous practice you learn to live in the thought that you are spirit, that you are not your body, you will gradually learn to function only from the Spiritual, and "the Satan of the senses" will "come" and find "nothing in you." "As a man thinketh in his heart," says Solomon, "so is he." In other words, sustained thought, perpetually suggesting in one direction, to the subconscious mind, will externalize in your life, and build you up in the direction of your thought. The moral issues of life lie in thought-control, and all spiritual growth is a deeper consciousness of God.

> " O God within my breast,
> Almighty ever-present Deity,
> Life that in me has rest,
> Whilst I, undying Life, have Power in Thee."

" O God within my Breast." Hold that thought of Emily Brontë's, know that the body and its claims are not yourself. The body provides the walls of the Temple in which dwells the Spirit, but it is not you. Claim boldly, by a mental act, the fullness of the inheritance of your true being in God. Always look for good in yourself and in others. Keep on affirming good. Evil is not a concrete entity, it is a symptom, not a fact, a symptom of non-realization of spirit. Realize the Spirit, yield to the promptings of the Spirit, Paul says, in this morning's Epistle, " Even so now yield." You know that the Spirit is in you, yield to it, cause it to rejoice, not to grieve. As you have yielded to the lower allurement, now yield to the higher. If you insist upon limiting your mental apprehension to rudimentary conceptions, then by all means go to confession and try to mitigate the anger you imagine God feels against you. The rubric indicates that confession to a priest is for those who "cannot quiet their own conscience," in other words, who will not use the Keys to the Kingdom of Heaven within them. But if you know that you are part of the boundless consciousness of Infinite life, if you know that by an effort of will you can blend your mind with universal mind, if you have found God as ever present Divine Love, Whose relationship to you as an individual life-centre in whom He is seeking to realize Himself is the closest, the tenderest, the surest, then you will need no external absolution, your one aim will be not to grieve the Spirit.

It is difficult to prescribe for others, but if ever you have times when you are crushed with sorrow, when memories are vivid and your eyes are full of tears, and no human being can comfort you, just mentally open your whole self inwardly and outwardly to the Soul of Souls. Go straight to the Divine. Say over and over again, "I am part of Infinite Spirit. Infinite Spirit, Thou shalt realize Thyself in me, I will not grieve Thee. Thy life is now pulsing through me. I will be a pure dwelling-place for Thy life. I am in touch now with the Power that made the universe. I claim now for myself, for my loved ones, for all, the fullness of our inheritance in Thee. I believe that measureless Love indwells all souls in whatever world they may be. Heaven and earth are full of Thy glory."

Believe me, there is no sorrow so profound, no sin-memory so deeply branded, that it cannot be transformed by this mental process of conscious identification with Infinite Spirit. Paul knew it, and in the knowledge of it he wrote that immortal sentence, "There is one God, and Father of all, Who is above all, and through all, and in all." And when we know that this Universal, Paternal, Transcendent, Omnipresent, and Immanent God is just as personally present with us on this planet as He is in the highest heaven, we can be patient with the conditions of this life, and look forward with reverent eagerness to the higher life which will be ours when we drop the body as some worn-out garment.

Sir Edwin Arnold in his paraphrase of the Bhagavadgita, well expresses it—

"For what is death?
'Tis but as when one layeth
His worn-out robes away,
And taking new ones sayeth,
These will I wear to-day.
So putteth by the Spirit
Lightly its garb of flesh,
And passeth to inherit
A residence afresh."

# THE WITNESS OF THE SPIRIT

"If thou hadst known."—LUKE xix. 42.

A PROFOUND truth underlies this exclamation of our Lord recorded in this morning's gospel,[1] and the whole of the pathetic incident, describing God in Christ weeping over Jerusalem, illustrates recent utterances which have brought me many thoughtful questions.

The theses I have laid down are, (1) that we are never unforgiven by Infinite Mind, that the only emotion excited in Infinite Mind by our wrong-doing is grief, and therefore Paul says "grieve not the Spirit." (2) That an intelligent analysis of man establishes a restful universalism so far as the ultimate issue of life's education for each separate human entity is concerned. Man is complex, he has within him three functioning centres, one of which is wholly and irrevocably omnipotent. Man is spirit, soul, and body. Spirit is the seat of his God-consciousness. Soul is the seat of his

[1] Tenth Sunday after Trinity.

Self-consciousness. Body is the seat of his sense-consciousness. In the spirit God dwells, in the soul self dwells, in the body sense dwells. Spirit influences body through soul, which is the seat of conscious mind. Harmony lies in soul, of which conscious mind is the functioning power, seeking its life and happiness by thinking itself into conscious oneness with spirit, the divinity within. Then, as soul will be no longer functioning from the plane of material conditions and sense impressions, physical body will obey mind ruled by spirit and the man will not sin.

This thesis establishes beyond cavil ultimate universal restitution upon an irrefragable basis, because spirit is God Immanent, spirit is omnipotent and infallible, the predestined purpose of spirit, though capable of being resisted and, considered in our time relation, delayed, can never be defeated. A man may so wreck his life here as to be practically derelict, he may have to go to school after school, but wherever he goes spirit goes with him ; it is not possible to exhaust the resources of spirit; "If I go down into hell, Thou art there," tireless, patient, remedial, deeply-grieved, but always waiting for recognition, and ultimately irresistible, for the fulfilment of each man's destiny is implicit in our Lord's words, which are not a command, but a prophecy, "Ye shall bc perfect, as your Father in heaven is perfect."

Now the irrational suggestion is made that this absolute confidence in the ultimate perfection of even the very worst encourages careless living, and indifference to present experiences. The criticism is shallow, and the incident recorded in this morning's gospel destroys it.

Man, national or individual, must be the product of his own development, his character must be his own manufacture. The fact that one of his functioning centres is divine, silences any complaint of injustice as to this obligation. True, he finds within him animal tendencies and hereditary warps that may lead him into breaches of the moral law; he is not responsible for these tendencies; he found them in his nature. Re-incarnationists say that he is responsible because he made that character in a previous incarnation. Common sense rebels against the suggestion. It would be grossly unjust that a man should inherit an evil character formed in a previous incarnation without also inheriting the experience of that incarnation to help him in the next. No, the responsibility for the carnal taint is not ours. It is true of all, as it was of the Christ, "a body hast Thou prepared me." Infinite Mind knows exactly how He has "body-formed" each one of us, and no one has the right to complain of what he finds in his body-self, because of the vast superiority of his spirit-self. Growth and education are through resistance; therefore the exact amount of body-resistance necessary to build us into saints is within us; but also within us is a power sufficient to conquer temptations a thousandfold greater. It remains for us to find that power, to know it, to use it. When we will not find it and use it we reap, in much suffering, what we have sown. No extra-cosmic world-ruler intervenes to prevent effects following causes, and Infinite Immanent Mind grieves or rejoices in each one of His human vehicles, in proportion as He is ignored or known. In to-day's gospel the drama is, as it were, acted out on the human stage for our edification. We see human life-centres reaping what they had sown, and Spirit "grieving" in the Person of Jesus, unable to intervene to avert consequences. "If thou hadst known," He says. That is, if, in the individual, will had constrained conscious mind which is soul, to discover and become absorbed in spirit, body would have obeyed, and these sorrows would have been averted. Jesus did not come to found a new religion, He aimed at spiritualizing Judaism.

He did not teach a new faith. "He lived and died," as Professor McGiffert says, "a loyal Jew, steeped in the traditions of His race, proud of its heritage, devoted to its ideals," but the lack of spiritual consciousness on the part of the leaders of Jewish thought blinded the nation, "they did not know." Jesus pleaded it for them when they murdered Him "They do not know what they are doing."

"If thou hadst known," He cried. As a true patriot, loving the city of His ancestors, deeply sympathizing with the populace left in blindness by their priests, He wept because the wilful ignorance of the leaders of the people made the catastrophe of the destruction of Jerusalem, and its attendant horrors, inevitable. There is truth in that old saying of the Cornish fishermen, "He who will not be ruled by the rudder must be ruled by the rock," and Jesus wept because Israel chose to be "ruled by the rock." Do those tears of Jesus over Jerusalem suggest the grief of the Spirit in any one of us because we will not mentally concentrate upon our spiritual potentiality? Man wills his own destiny so far as this life is concerned. He cannot defeat God's Will as to his ultimate destiny, but he can defeat it in these time relations. Professor Huxley said, "A human being, though a machine, is capable, within certain limits, of self-adjustment." Just so, and what is this capability of self-adjustment? It is spirit waiting for will to force conscious mind to recognize it and use it. It is the inner potentiality waiting to be "born from above" by being known and appealed to. If it were not there, no responsibility would attach to us; we should justifiably remain intelligent animals, living on the carnal plane. "Dwelt no power divine within us, how could God's Divineness win us?" But it does dwell within us, and its function is to direct the whole man through his conscious mind as my brain directs my hand. When you know this, you have made the great discovery. You cannot express it in words, any more than you can define love by mathematics. It is the Divine functioning power which, when known, enables you to see through the apparent into the real, and control the whole man. It is the "secret of the Lord," and the "secret of the Lord" is the recognition, not only that there is a "soul in all things and that soul is God," but also that the cosmic consciousness which constitutes the pulse of life in all things is specially and peculiarly self-conscious in man, as Infinite Mind seeking vehicles for self-realization.

"If thou hadst known," said our Lord. Yes, if we had always known, in the past, we should have been saved some heartaching memories now. The incidents of average human life without this knowledge are not unlike the moaning of the wind through a mass of suspended telegraph wires; the secret of the wire is hidden in its heart, invisible, inaudible. Through it are flashing messages, words of love and wisdom and power, while the outside eye sees only the tangle of the mass of wires, and the outside ear hears only the moaning of the wind through the wires. That is life with its sorrows to those who do not know spirit within them. How are we to know? Again I repeat by using the will to hold the conscious mind to the assurance that Spirit, Omnipotent, Omniscient, does dwell in us always, and, though this assurance will not necessarily become a continuous sense-experience, it will, after practice, be so intuitively established, that you will know how to rally to it, and you will be able to speak to spirit within you and say, "I know Thy thoughts and Thy power are seeking expression within me. I know that Thou art my truest, deepest being."

Certain inferences follow. If you know the truth of the three functioning centres in man, and the supreme superiority of the spirit-centre, you recognize that the struggle within you, and the painful consciousness of failure within you, are the consequence of the activity of spirit, always raising, unknown to us, a standard within us, in contrast with which, actions that are prompted by mind and body alone are imperfect. By the experience of this contrast we are being educated. Paul states it boldly: "The creature was made subject to vanity," that is, to the discipline of these contrasts, "not willingly, but by reason of Him." That is by reason of spirit enfleshing itself in matter.

Then again the knowledge of this cosmic consciousness, that God "sleeps in the stone, dreams in the plant, wakens in the animal, and is self-conscious in man," gives a new significance to matter. Matter is not an illusion projected from our own minds; matter is a veritable garment of God. They who consider matter an illusion forget that the conception of an Infinite God must include matter. As the earth-spirit in Faust says—

"So at the roaring loom of time I ply
And weave for God the garment that thou seest Him by."

The study of everything in the external world serves to suggest and to stimulate the greater things in man's invisible world of thought and feeling, "The Kingdom of Heaven within him." From these garments of matter, from these common phenomena of our earthly lives, Immanent Spirit is constantly appealing to us to find the spirit-meaning beneath them. Once before, the Lord Jesus, the unique specialization of Immanent Spirit, spoke those suggestive words, "If thou hadst known." It was to the woman of Samaria at the well of Sychar. "If thou hadst known," He said, "Who it was that said unto thee, 'Give Me to drink,' thou wouldst have asked of Him, and He would have given thee living water." In other words, thou wouldst have seen beneath the material incident a spiritual meaning.

"If thou hadst known." Do I know? Can I know? How can I know? Do the things which belong to my peace depend upon the development of my brain power? Is it only the aristocrats of the intellect who will enter into the fruition of the Beatitude, "This is life eternal, that they may know Thee"? Though the brain is useful—for the sequences of moral and religious truth involve processes of reasoning, and a theology that could not stand the test of logic would be self-condemned—the knowledge spoken of here is a higher, profounder wisdom than brain wisdom.

Remember that there are within us two originating founts of Knowledge. Paul differentiated them sharply as, one, the "carnal mind," meaning the intellect alone, and the other the "Christ mind," meaning the Spirit ruling the intellect.

Paul says that the "natural man," that is the man doing his thinking on the intellectual plane alone, "receiveth not the things of the Spirit, for they are foolishness unto him; neither can he know them, for they are spiritually discerned." Well, have I no spiritual discernment? Of course I have. God thought-generated me, the real me, in His own image and likeness, and God is Spirit, so I am spirit. Infinite Mind has thought me into terrestrial birth, and has implanted me in an hereditary flesh nature.

My hereditary flesh nature is soul in which is intellect, and body in which is appetite. But is that all of me? No indeed. There is in me a potentiality of wisdom, inherited from Infinite Mind, which awaits the action of my will upon my thought-faculty to become awakened spiritual consciousness ruling the whole man. I cannot form a mental concept of Infinite Mind because I can only form an intellectual concept of anything by mentally differentiating it from something else. I cannot, therefore, think Infinite Mind because there is nothing from which, or from whom, I can mentally differentiate Him, and yet I know Him by this inner knowledge, this spiritual consciousness, with an intensity of conviction that needs no logical syllogism to justify it. No man can describe to another this inner intuitive knowledge. No man can speak or write of that which Browning calls "the immortal centre in us all where truth abides in fullness." It is "the secret of the Lord," the faculty of spiritual discernment which enables us to know that all visible things are sacraments of spirit; that every incident of the commonest daily life thinly veils a divine meaning for us; that Spirit is perpetually appealing to us; that a lily, a rose, a sparrow, a pain, a headache, an anxiety, are God's sermons; that a strange prophet in our street, as at Jerusalem, a wayfarer asking for water by a well-side, as at Sychar, are disguises of spirit seeking to teach us something. That a crisis calling for decision in our daily life, a summons to duty which puts principle to the test, an appeal to our generosity, kindness, self-control, are not mere chance, but the operation of this Infinite Cosmic Mind haunting our lives in love, that He may develop our characters, and lead us, without forcing us, to seek "the things which belong to our peace."

Try and see life from this standpoint. If, for example, we had only known, when perhaps we sharply refused some request, when we petulantly wounded some heart that loved us, when we unreasonably misunderstood some speech or action of another, when we shrank from the truth that crucifies, and sought refuge in the lie that shields, if we had known that Spirit was appealing to us in that opportunity, that it was He Who was suggesting that action, that self-control, that sacrifice! If we had judged incidents from the spirit rather than from the flesh, we should have strengthened ourselves, and helped others.

The final thought is this. It is well to form the habit of knowing that spirit is in everything that happens to us. Dismiss the delusion that matter is not, and that God knows nothing of matter. Matter, incidents, material conditions, life experiences, are spirit's media through which He speaks to us. "Verily Thou art a God that hidest Thyself," said the prophet; but it is only His intense nearness that hides Him; and as He is everywhere, and always Love everywhere, we can mentally find Him in every hiding-place, and we can say with Cowper—

> "In the vast, and in the minute, we see
> The unambiguous footsteps of the God
> Who gives its lustre to the insect's wing,
> And wheels His Throne upon the rolling worlds."

That we can obtain this mental attitude, that

we can reach to this divine "knowledge centre" within us, is implied by the fact that we must do it, it is why we are body-formed in this world. Spirit grieves when we will not do it. Jesus wept over Israel because they would not do it.

It is the old injunction. The process is by becoming thought-immersed in spirit, mentally losing yourself in God. It is, at certain periods of solitude, to close the conscious mind to all theories, theologies, definitions, accommodations, externals, symbols, and just be alone with God the Spirit, *solus cum solo*. Relax the body, and still the mind; blend the conscious mind with the Infinite Mind, and then stop thinking. When you do that you are dwelling for the time in the "secret place of the Most High." You are "abiding under the Shadow of the Almighty." While you are thus mentally dwelling in "the secret place," no sorrow can touch you, no anxiety can fret you; you are in full communion with the spirit beings on the other side; you are in vital union with the Infinite, Omnipotent, Originating Father-Spirit. While abiding under the Shadow of the Almighty you cannot hear the roar of the machinery of the world, to your material duties in which world you must presently return. You are in peace, for "Thou shalt keep him in perfect peace whose mine is stayed on Thee."

## DON'T WORRY

"Be not anxious for your life."—MATT. vi. 25.

THE most literal translation of the Greek is " don't worry " about your life. You cannot add a cubit to your stature, He says, by worrying. Three times, within a few verses, He repeats those words, *me merimnate*, don't worry. Now it is intensely significant to notice upon what foundation our Lord bases that injunction not to worry. When we, humble followers, take this same foundation, they call us Pantheists, because they will not understand Paul's glorious affirmation in Ephesians iv. 6. God, Paternal, Transcendent, Omnipresent, Immanent.

Our Lord takes us to Infinite Immanent Mind. He talks of birds and flowers and grass, and suggests that the perfect harmony in nature should give us a restful sense of oneness with the Soul of the Universe, of Whom birds and flowers and grass are self-expressions on a lower plane of livingness. He wants us to realize that the whole creation is permeated by an Omniscient Intelligence, and that we humans are justified in transferring this conception from the plane of the universal to the plane of the particular, in our individual lives, and resting in the fact that we are part of the Infinite life, and of more value than many birds and many flowers.

I remember when my friend Frank Buckland, the great naturalist, was passing over, that thought came into his mind. Probably he was quite unconscious that he was quoting the Sermon on the Mount. He said, "I am sure that the God Who has taken such care of the little fishes will not fail in His goodness to Her Majesty's inspector of fisheries when he passes out of the body." We humans worry because we don't think deeply enough into the philosophy of life. As Bacon said, "A little philosophy inclineth men's minds to atheism, but depth of philosophy bringeth men's minds to true religion." And this is the mystic meaning of the words in this morning's Gospel, "Launch out into the deep."

So our Lord says "consider," "think," "be still and know," and you won't worry.

In speaking of the flowers, you remember the Lord chooses the lily. We all have our favourite flowers, the lily was probably His. I have recorded my thoughts about the lily in a previous publication, but it would be the same if He had said consider the rose—the rose speaks to me personally far more than the lily.

If we were capable of really "considering" a rose, by the laws of philosophic thought, and knowing how it grew, we should discover the whole history of life in that flower. If we could trace it back to its first beginning, we should have solved the riddle of life, and discovered, as Tennyson said of the "little flower in the crannied wall," the secret of God and man. To "consider," therefore, deeply, any flower, is to be led to those thoughts that, as Wordsworth says, "lie too deep for tears." It is to bring Infinite Mind very near, it is to bring the whole man into unison with the supreme source of life, for a flower is a thought of God; its fragrance, its beauty of form, represent an eternal idea in the Mind of the Universal Spirit. The life in the flower is the same in kind, though not the same in degree, as the expression of Universal Spirit in you and in me. Every flower is a Sacrament of God, an affirmation of the beautiful Mind of Him in Whom "we live and move and have our being"; and that beautiful Mind is the Spirit Who is described as "brooding upon the face of the waters" before the etheric atoms were concentrated into form, and order came from chaos. So it is as a symbol of ourselves that our Lord bids us think of a flower as an antidote to worry. He would have us realize that even a flower is the unfolding of a vast Divine plan, conceived in the timeless womb of the Infinite Mind, and He would have us draw the inference that the cosmic Intelligence in the flower is the same evolutionary principle which finds its highest self-recognition in man, and man's unceasing stimulus to strive after the higher life, and his justification for tranquil confidence in the Love of God in the midst of the perplexities of the world, consist in the fact that God is not ruling him from without, but slowly evolving within him the character which from all eternity He has purposed, just as the inner principle of life in the plant slowly evolves the perfect flower.

Therefore He says don't worry about your life. The only thing we may worry about is our attitude towards life, and that is where we differ from the rose.

Though a universal intelligence permeates nature, inherent in every one of its manifestations, there is a profound difference between the atomic intelligence in the flower, and the individual intelligence in the man. The action of the cosmic mind in the flower is automatic, its growth and beauty are the unreflecting result of the continuous adjustment of internal relations to external relations. Man's evolution must be by intelligent individual volition. "We are men," says Tennyson, "strong in will, to strive, to seek, to find, and not to yield." Our life, like the life of the flower, is from within. It is Divine; but it must be helped by our own individual intelligence and effort. That which in the flower is mechanical and subconscious, must be with us a conscious exercise of the individual will directing the thoughts. We are not responsible for where we are planted. "My Father is the Husbandman." The environment into which I am born is His affair, not mine; and men, like flowers, have not the same environments to overcome, or the same difficulties to meet. When I have spoken of the lily I have always emphasized the example of the water-lily, whose whole growth is a continuous struggle; the water-lily must rise from the depths, and lift its head above the pressure around it, and then, resting on the surface of the very difficulty it has overcome, it opens out its golden petals and feeds upon the sunshine. But the water-lily does this automatically, by the "power that worketh in it." Its means of rising are calculated exactly according to the depth of the water in which natural law has planted it. "There hath no temptation taken it," so to speak, "but such as it shall be able to overcome."

As I have pointed out—and I love to repeat the analogy—there is within the stem of the water-lily an apparatus, consisting of an elastic spiral coil, which expands and contracts, giving it power to rise or sink as the water deepens or diminishes, so that it may be always just sufficiently above the pressure in which it lives, and face to face with the life-giving sun. That spiral coil is, of course, subconscious cosmic mind responding to the suggestion of the need of the moment. Our spiral coil, "the power that works in us," demands the initiative of our conscious minds.

It is for us to work with God, to set our moral capacity in activity by our will. How can we work with God? We can mentally make our environment. We can train the conscious mind so to rest in the Divine Love that we refuse to worry when things seem to go wrong. We can mentally rest in "the secret place of the Most High." We can live in the promise, "He shall hide thee privily in His Own presence from the provoking of all men, He shall keep thee secretly in His tabernacle from the strife of tongues." But, mark, if we will not mentally stay in that tabernacle, how can He hide us? If we choose to join in the strife of tongues, how can He keep us? Peter has something to say about tongues in this morning's Epistle, though he takes the rather low ground of material comfort, but it is the same on the spiritual plane—

> Every word has its own sphere,
> True or false, that never dies,
> Every word man's lips have uttered
> Echoes in God's skies.

And as God's skies are within us, for "the Kingdom of Heaven is within you," joining in the strife of tongues, readiness to repeat a scandal and so keep it alive, will externalize in our own lives, and we shall have made our own environment to our own great disadvantage. Remember the Oriental maxim—

"To be angry with another is to punish yourself for his fault."

So, while bidding us not to worry about our lives, Our Lord plainly indicates that our growth cannot be mechanical, like the growth of the flower. He speaks of two masters, the two natures within us, the Kingdom of Heaven within us, and the carnal nature in which the Kingdom of Heaven is enshrined. And the severity of the contrast between these two, between duty and inclination, desire and self-control, temper and gentleness, in other words, God and Mammon, is the measure of the growth of the higher man. If the will, the intention, the whole power of the conscious mind is resolutely thrown on the side of the Divine force working within, God's human plant rises above the lower tendencies and the narrower life, and, like the water-lily, whose spiral coil has lifted it above, and caused to rest upon, the environment that seemed to hinder it, the growing soul utilizes the natural tendencies as helps to force the whole man Godwards. It is a matter of mental training. Therefore, if I find myself worrying, I had better ask myself the question, Is the Divine nature thus lifting me? Am I claiming it? using it? The power we do not exert, like the limb we do not exercise or the faculty we do not expand, slumbers, weakens, finally atrophies.

The first necessity, then, is to believe intensely that Divine Mind is "the power that worketh in us," and the next is to suffer that power to manifest. The saying about not "toiling and spinning" has reference only to the evolution of the Christ character. It means that the Christ character is not a Mosaic of moralities, painfully built up in imitation of a stainless model, but a life; not hand-made, like Solomon's robes, but God-evolved, like the flower's beauty. It is no encouragement to idleness on the human plane; it is the clear, obvious duty of man on the material plane to toil and spin, and take thought for the morrow ; to provide, for himself and others, food and clothing. His garments will not grow on him, and his food will not fall from heaven into his mouth. " Men must work, and women must weep," yes, and work too, but man's character will be a growth from within.

It is very important that this should be clear to us. Immanent Infinite Mind is shaping and guiding every event, and opportunity, and trial, and disappointment in these lives of ours, towards a definite end. But its working is conditioned by our receptivity. It is for us to watch for it, to conform to it, to live as recognizing it, to be constantly blending our mind with Infinite Mind, to strive to live purely, nobly, kindly, helpfully, self-forgetfully, in the common duties and daily frictions of ordinary life, as vehicles of God's self-realization. And it is in this willing, intelligent fellow-working with the Divine Nature within that God's human flowers grow.

Then we have nothing to be anxious about except our own mental attitude towards the facts of life. The Lord says, " Be not anxious about your life." Then most certainly be not anxious about your death. Some good people are so afraid of death. Dying is going home, returning whence we came. Wordsworth is right—

> "Not in entire forgetfulness and not in utter nakedness,
> But trailing clouds of glory do we come from God,
> Who is our home."

Dying will be going home, and "there is no place like home." Many are longing for that home, they suffer from what the Germans call Heimweh, "home sickness." While there must be no cowardly pining to get away, the transitory nature of these material conditions, and the emptiness of the world when the best loved have left it, destroy any idea of a "home" here. That was the pressure that forced from the heart of John Howard Payne his touching song of "Home, sweet, home." For forty years he had known no home of his own, and he died in lonely lodgings in Paris. Well, we are all in "lonely lodgings" here, when our best friends have gone home, but they have only gone home a little before us. Our Lord said: "If ye loved Me, ye would rejoice, because I go to the Father." He meant that understanding love would patiently reach beyond the frontier of this world, and though doomed to temporary loneliness, would, in its inmost, rejoice that the dear spirit has gone home, and would say to it:

"Thank God, thou hadst the peace and I the lifelong pain." There is no need to worry about our death any more than about our life, and there is no need to worry about the death of our dearest friends.

God is Love, and God is everywhere. In the perfume of a rose, in the brain of a philosopher, in the specialization in Jesus. A flower, with its beautiful form and delicate perfume, is the assurance of the sensitiveness of the Soul of the Universe to the perfect development of even the smallest of the multitudinous manifestations in which He has expressed Himself. Therefore, we, the higher manifestations, need not fear. "Are not ye," says our Lord, "much better than they?" We cannot penetrate the secret of how Creative Thought is transmuted into phenomena, animate and inanimate; but the Immanence of God, which dreams its lovely dream in the flower, is intensely self-conscious in man. And to discover this truth, to draw the correct inference from it, is to have gained a freedom from worry. It is to "rest in the Lord," in the assurance that measureless love, linked to omnipotent purpose, enspheres our whole being. Of course, it does not mean freedom from educative heart-aches and tears. It is not "from" all these things, but "in" all these things, that, when we know God, we are "more than conquerors." Jesus, the perfect illustration of the Immanence of God, endured the Cross, and His brow was furrowed both with personal pain and the heavy burden of the sorrows of others. But I am certain that He never worried. I suggest, then, that a true mental effort to live in conscious oneness with Infinite Spirit will lift the burden of fear, and of anticipation of trouble, from our hearts. When you wake in the morning and are once more consciously present with God, your first thought should be, "Abba Father, I am resting in Thee. To-day is the to-morrow for which Thou didst yesterday bid me take no thought." And then say: "Our Father, give me a deeper consciousness of my oneness with Thee to-day than I have ever had before; give me wisdom and love in doing Thy work to-day; help me to evolve from my life this day all that Thou hast involved in it; let me know that I have within me Thy Mind, Thy Spirit, and that Thou art helping me to grow into 'the measure of the stature of the fullness of Christ.'"

Now, please do not say that you cannot train your conscious mind into this attitude of auto-suggestion. You can. Every one can. But, while learning it, don't be discouraged because you don't feel it. Believe that the Immanence of the Divine Mind in you is an irrefragable philosophic fact, and act upon it as if you did realize it. Make an affirmation: "The Lord says my life is one with the Infinite Life. He spoke to me about flowers, and birds, and grass. He wanted me to know that the wonderful universal livingness shining in the sun, budding in the flower, glowing in the insect's wing, pulsing in the ether and sending its vibrations to distant worlds, is in me as Divine Consciousness. He wanted me to know that the Infinite Mind is realizing Himself in me. I will believe it, though it is not, as yet, a sense-impression, and I will claim it and act upon it as if I did feel it." That affirmation sustained, will externalize in your life, and you will marvel at the power in yourself which it will awaken and call into activity. And if the lack of realization continues, what then? Well, what does common sense suggest that we should do? When under some physical weakness, some mental strain, some crushing sorrow, some tares showing themselves in your special wheat-field, darkness settles down, just endure. "Stand fast in the Lord," believe without seeing. Say, with intention, "Thine is the Kingdom, and the power, and the glory." "All things work together for good for them that love God." We shall, of course, have our dark moments; the Lord Jesus had His dark moment on Calvary. If we have a dark moment this week, call to mind that Voice that told us not to worry. He says: "Be not anxious for your life"; "go out, if you can, into the fields, behold the birds, consider the flowers; I am immanent in them, are ye not much better than they?" And if the darkness is not at once removed, still don't worry. Take your place by the side of Job in his darkest hour. It is one of the grandest utterances recorded in the Bible: "Behold I go forward and He is not there, and backward, but I cannot perceive Him. He hideth Himself that I cannot see Him, but, He knoweth the way that I take, and, when He hath tried me, I shall come forth as gold."

## VICARIOUS SACRIFICE

Bring no price, God's love is free,
To Paul, to Magdalen, to me.

"But while he was yet afar off, his Father saw him, and ran, and fell on his neck, and kissed him."—LUKE XV. 20.

HAVE we ever reflected what this allegory involves as to our relation with the All-originating Infinite Mind?

Lack of recognition of its meaning has warped human thinking, receptivity of its message irradiates life with inward peace. It is an authoritative picture of the real attitude of the Creating Spirit towards the individual life-centres in which He is immanent. None of the great pre-Christian religions of the world, which have in their measure interpreted the thought-transcending Infinite Mind, have been able thus to realize that Love, and only Love, is the prime moving power of the Creating Spirit; it is the consummation of the Christ revelation in its fundamental aspect, and who with this self-painted portrait of the Father-

God before him, can mentally cling to the rudimentary conception that God needs reconciling to man?

I recently emphasized the axiom that everything must take form in thought before the thought could take form in the thing. We humans had thought-form in Infinite Mind before the thought of Infinite Mind took body-form in individual lives. As God said to Jeremiah the prophet, "Before I formed thee in the womb I knew thee." He "body-formed" us into terrestrial life that we might come to ourselves, and so come to Him. We can only be conscious of anything by realizing some relation between ourselves and it. We could only become conscious of God by realizing ourselves as individuals, and being mentally separated from God, that we might, of ourselves, come back to God, from Whom, essentially, in our inmost, we had never been separated.

This coming back to God, St. Paul tells us, is a mental act, a change in thinking: "Be ye transformed by the renewing of your mind."

It is a coming to yourself, your real self, the self that lies buried under material conditions and hereditary wrong thinking, a bondage to which we were "made subject," says St. Paul, "not by our own will but by God." The problem of life consists in realizing our true relation to the Infinite Spirit and then striving to live up to the realization, and the first step towards this is complete satisfaction as to the attitude of the Infinite Spirit towards ourselves. This is essential, because the power of Infinite Mind to realize Himself in us, and help us to externalize in our lives His ideal of us, which He loved before He made us, is conditioned by our appreciation of what He is in Himself. Now, our mental conception of what God is in Himself is obviously dominated by inherited mental images and conceptions which are the result of quite honest natural thinking upon the surface plane of earth experience. Paul tells us that the universal order of thought is "first that which is natural, afterwards that which is spiritual." It is quite in accord with this revealed order of thought that human minds should first conceive of God as an external World-Ruler, approach to Whom could only be by propitiatory amenities of various kinds, and that when spiritual consciousness awakens the old conception should fade. God is revealed to man in modes adapted to different stages in power of realization. Mental conceptions suitable to one stage are intended to be surpassed in another stage, and it is only natural that these conceptions should overlap each other. For example, one complete theological system has arisen from the fact that Augustine, who though an enthusiastic Platonist before his baptism by Ambrose in the fourth century, was untouched by the spiritual Neo-Platonism which leavened the catechetical school of Alexandria, built his religion upon the theory of objective Deism. According to this conception an infinite indebtedness had been incurred by man to the objective World-Ruler, and the suffering and death of a sinless Victim was exacted as the only expiation acceptable by an Omnipotent Abstraction called Justice. Anselm, the Latin Archbishop of Canterbury in the eleventh century, reduced the teaching of Augustine to strict dogmatic definition, and this conception, based upon the principle, "first that which is natural," was obviously adapted to a certain stage of perception, and has proved a useful working hypothesis. It has led many, under the fear of Divine punishment, to cling with yearning gratitude to God's Pacifier, the Saviour of the world, and to lead new lives. To those whose minds are in that sphere of understanding this conception is still of value. And for all thus awakened and thus reformed we thank God. But under increasing spiritual consciousness we cannot silence the question: Is it the highest conception of our relation to the Infinite Mind? Can it be traced in any of Our

Lord's recorded words ? Is there a hint of it in the Parable of the Prodigal Son, the immortal self-painted portrait of Almighty God ? Is it consistent with the truth of Divine Immanence ?

I speak of it to-day because our Liturgy, derived mainly from Augustinian sources, even our beautiful consecration prayer, contains many suggestions of this conception of propitiation, and also because at this season stress is laid upon the sacrificial aspect of Our Blessed Lord's death upon the Cross. The programme for Lent is "Look and think." "Behold and see if there be any sorrow like unto My sorrow." But what is the interpretation of the programme ? St Paul tells us. It is that by "beholding we may be transformed into the same image." Realized identity with the Divine Victim is the object to be attained, and that, not by copying a model, or accepting a sacrifice, but by sharing a life ; not by intellectually assenting to an historic fact, and appropriating personal benefit therefrom, but by the evolution of a similar character. Our Lord Jesus was both the representative of man, and the manifestation of God. He explained to man the problem of himself, and He revealed God to man. In the first aspect He was the visible embodiment, in absolute perfection, of a Divine Immanence which is not limited to

His single personality, but is the possession of every member of humanity. Thus was He the ideal specimen of the race, the assurance, the guarantee of the essential divinity of humanity, which He asserted when He spoke of God as " your Father and My Father." In the second aspect He was the visible specialization of the moral qualities of the Infinite Mind, Himself for ever invisible. In the first aspect He taught humanity where to find and how to approach God, He spoke of God as " the Father in Him." In the second aspect He illustrated in Himself the method of this Immanence of God in human life-centres, and in the complete manifestation He was the at-one-ment between the human and the Divine. This teaching differentiated Christianity from the previous Judaic conception. Whereas the Jewish religion provided elaborate methods whereby the wrath of the Deity might be propitiated, the fundamental basis of Christianity is that the Infinite Mind, being one with humanity, needs no propitiation except the propitiation of His yearning for perfect vehicles for His self-manifestation in His sons, and that His sole and inexorable demand upon His children is the sacrifice of the human partial will to His indwelling and perfect Will.

The idea of propitiation was not the earliest

conception of sacrifice. The earliest idea of sacrifice was Eucharistic, not propitiatory. In the most ancient Vedic hymns man is represented as essentially one with his fellow-man, with Nature, and with the Divine Source of Nature; and sacrifice was not a propitiatory offering, but a feast in which the Infinite Spirit became the guest of man. And in generating the sacrificial flame by the friction of two pieces of wood, man was considered to be evoking, under his own hand, the Immanent Divine principle; and his offering of bread and wine, partly consumed by himself and his fellow-man, and partly ascending by combustion, was a symbol of human life blending with, and uniting its strength to, the cosmic Immanence. When the sacrifice was animal, its significance lay, not in the death of the animal, but in the Eucharistic meal which followed; it was considered to be a meal shared with the divinity. In earliest times a portion of the meal was placed in groves or sacred places, with the idea that the deity would consume it. As more spiritualized views of Dyaush-Pitar, the "World Father," prevailed, the portion for the deity was etherealized by fire, and thus discharged into the air, that the "sweet smell and savour" might ascend. Gradually, as the conception of objective Deism prevailed, new ideas of sacrifice obtained; the offering became a gift or tribute to an external deity, and from this was slowly evolved the conception of propitiating the "World-Father." This conception once established, it followed that the propitiating power of a sacrifice was measured by the magnitude of the gift; and as a human being was more precious than an animal, human sacrifices, in times of great distress, became the custom.

The tenacity with which this hereditary wrong-thinking lingered in the Judaic theology is evidenced by the hideous human sacrifice related in the twenty-first chapter of the Second Book of Samuel, where seven innocent men, grandsons of Saul, were "hanged before the Lord" to avert a famine in the land. The student can trace the slow transformation of the Eucharistic idea of sacrifice into the expiatory, and note how, under the Jewish sacerdotalism, the notion of averting the anger of Jahveh became the one predominant idea of sacrifice. The more inspired of the prophets protested unceasingly, but unavailingly, against the propitiatory idea. David cries out, "Thou desirest no sacrifice, else would I give it Thee." Samuel says, "To obey is better than sacrifice." Isaiah says, "The Lord delighteth not in burnt offerings." Jeremiah says, "I, Jehovah, commanded not your fathers concerning sacrifices." Hosea says, "I will have mercy and not sacrifice." Amos says, "God hateth their sacrifices." Micah says, "Will the Lord be pleased with thousands of rams, what doth the Lord require of thee but to do justly and love mercy and walk humbly with thy God?" But the traditional conception was rooted in the human mind, and the Infinite Father-Spirit accepted the instinct as a loving earthly father will accept from a child some intrinsically worthless gift. He regulated it through Moses and his successors, purified and checked it through the prophets, and finallysatisfied it for ever on Calvary, for those who still clung to the conception inherited from the blood shed on heathen altars, so that timid hearts, who still hankered after propitiation, might take refuge in that interpretation, and have "boldness to enter into the holiest."

The true scope and nature of the sacrifice of Christ is luminously expressed in the tenth chapter of the Epistle to the Hebrews, emphatically contradicting the conception of propitiation, and asserting that the only sacrifice imperatively demanded by God is a yielded will, and a forcible change of thinking. Read it, and see if there is any possibility of confusion in its interpretation. "For it is impossible that the blood of bulls and of goats should take away sin; wherefore when He cometh into the world (that is, Jesus), He saith, Sacrifice and offering Thou wouldest not, but a body hast Thou prepared Me. Then said I, Lo, I am come to do Thy will, O God. He taketh away the first (that is, the conception of propitiatory sacrifice) that He may establish the second (that is the sacrifice of filial obedience to the will of God), by the which will we have been sanctified by the offering of the body of Jesus Christ once for all." In other words, the Perfect representative of the race atoned—at-one-ed—the limited human will to the universal Divine will, and so offered Himself without spot to God. And in this at-one-ment, through the organic spiritual identity of all human beings with the historic Christ, humanity is potentially at-one-ed to God through the attained perfection of one member of the race. Thus does a clearer view of the absolute identity of humanity with the historic Christ, and a deeper knowledge of the relation of man to Infinite Divine Love, clearly demonstrate that the only sacrifice man can offer to God is his own personal self-dedication. Thus does it convince that the atonement is not a single isolated propitiatory fact, but a demonstration, a symbol, of the process which takes place in the soul of each individual member of the race. Thus are we encouraged to discover and appeal to the God within us, and say, "Power that worketh in me, Mind of God embodied in Jesus and immanent in me, take me, break me, make me." Thus, when we "survey the wondrous Cross on which the Prince of Glory died," instead of shudderingly thanking Him for hanging there in our place, we shall realize that it is a manifestation of the Eternal passion of the Immanent God, and aim at recapitulating in ourselves the same perfectly yielded will, the same readiness to endure the cross, despising the shame, the same perfect at-one-ment of the human and the Divine ; and when, by "beholding, we have become transformed," and a higher, holier, purer life has blessed us, and our God-consciousness is awakened, and school-time is almost over, and home-coming near, for the same triumphant parting committal, "Father, into Thy hands I commend My Spirit."

But it may be asked is not "vicarious sacrifice" a truth universally recognized by the human conscience, and did not Jesus come to "save His people from their sins ?" Assuredly yes. The instinct of vicarious sacrifice is one of the strongest evidences of the Immanence of God, for the self-differentiation of Infinite

Mind in Creation is the symbol and the initiator of all self-sacrifice. The self-sacrifice of Captain Oates, who laid down his life for his friends, was a veritable ray of light from the Immanent God. His noble act has enriched and elevated humanity. As God " laid down His Life " in creation, he laid down his life for his brethren. The best human lives are made up of self-sacrifice for others, sacrifices of inclination, of time, of goods, of health, and, as in the case of Captain Oates, of life itself. But though these sacrifices are made for others, there is no conception in them of buying off the vengeance of a Supreme Power. The Lord Jesus, Who was " made in all things like unto His Brethren," lived a life of constant self-sacrifice for others, and His death upon the Cross was the crowning sacrifice for the one truth which can save the world. They crucified Him because He claimed Oneness with God for Himself, and for Humanity. Again, yes, assuredly, He came to "save His people from their sins," that was the meaning of His name, but how? By revealing, manifesting, demonstrating, causing men to recognize the divinity of Humanity. " Saving men from sins " does not mean saving men from the consequences of sin. It is an inexorable educative law that effects must follow causes. He saved men from their sins by showing them how, by right thinking as to their relation to the Infinite Spirit, they could be saved from sinning. It is only as a man becomes conscious of his own divinity, as he realizes in thought that he, individually, is an expression of the Immanent Spirit, that he really knows what sin is.

The sense of sin that seeks to hide under a propitiation is fear of punishment, not horror at profaning God's temple. The depth of the sense of sin is exactly proportioned to the soul's vision of the Immanence of God. The man who has realized his identity with the Infinite Life, and knows that the Divine Spirit dwells in him, if he falls into sin, suffers an agony of shame of which the believer in a propitiatory sacrifice is wholly incapable. He knows that no price except his own willing suffering can buy him out of that bondage. Until he is restored he has within him the enduring chastisement of a perpetual heartache, not because he is afraid of hell—he is in hell now—but because he has grieved, and knows that he has grieved, the God within him.

Jesus saves you from sin by saving you from sinning, and He saves you from sinning by claiming for you identity with Himself, and so assuring you of your own divinity. "I in them and Thou in Me," He said, meaning that the Godhead specialized in Him is potential and germinal in you. He saves you from sinning by training your thought to dwell habitually upon the transcendent fact that you are, in your measure, as He was in full measure, a vehicle in whom Infinite Spirit is realizing Himself, and that your body is "a temple of the Holy Ghost."

> "Know this, O Man, sole root of sin in thee
> Is not to know thine own divinity."

Therefore, inasmuch as we are bound to become what we see ourselves ideally to be, whoever teaches a man to realize that he is essentially divine, has saved that man from his sins. We cannot see into each other's hearts, but are we conscious of having thus grieved, profaned the divinity within us? Do we now realize with horror the revolting blasphemy that such action implies? Do we, in consequence of this realization, fear to face the blinding Purity of the Infinite Spirit? We need not. We can meet that fear with the Master-truth underlying the imperishable self-painted portrait of the creative Power Who loved us before He made us, and Who has recorded of Himself—

"And while he was yet afar off the Father

saw him, and ran, and fell on his neck and kissed him."

Verily " the Eternal God is our refuge, and underneath are the everlasting arms."

# PHILOSOPHICAL TRANSUBSTANTIATION

"If there is no Resurrection, then is not Christ risen."—I Cor. xv. 13.

According to St. Paul, then, resurrection is not a fact because Christ was raised, but Christ was raised because resurrection was a fact. The survival of the Christ, and His materializing Himself into visibility in the presence of many witnesses, has set the seal of positive certainty upon the age-long conviction of the immortality of those in whose nature is embodied the immortality of God, and, as Jesus stands for the race, we are now absolutely certain that—

"With the morn the Angel face will smile,
That we have loved long since and lost awhile."

I want to follow this thought of the immortality of God being embodied in our nature in a particular direction. There is one inference in this connection which seems to me specially to challenge attention.

This belief in One Infinite Life, of which Infinite Life we and our loved ones are part, fills us with a fearless rest. At the same time the immeasurableness of a universal creative consciousness is liable to be somewhat vague to the average finite mind, because Infinity must be impersonal, and as we are persons we hunger for Personality in God. Now, though the Universal Parent-Spirit is not a Person, there is nothing lacking in Him of all that we mean by Personality except outward form, and this natural craving for outward form, for Personality, in the Infinite Impersonal Mind, has been completely satisfied by a right understanding of the manifestation of God in our Lord Jesus Christ. He is the externalized embodiment, in one specially prepared life-centre, of the " personalness," and moral qualities, of the All-diffused Originating Spirit. When, therefore, with awakened spiritual eye, we see Jesus, we see God. " In Him dwells all the fullness of the Godhead bodily." He is God's answer to the philosophic problem of how mentally to specialize, personify, the universal Spirit, while at the same time mentally preserving its universality. Therefore the Lord Jesus is, in that sense, the Sacrament, or outward and visible Sign, the manifested "Personalness," of the inward spiritual Infinite Mind.

It follows that the Principle of a Sacrament, which is the focussing, the specializing in an external manifestation, in time and space relations, of a universal invisible power, is established in the Incarnation. Jesus was the Sacrament of God. Now no incident in the ministry of Jesus was more significant than His perpetuating the Sacramental Principle, and instituting the Holy Eucharist, as His last ministerial act, and it seems to me to be a kind of stagnation of the rational faculty, and a disoyalty to the philosophic estimate of the Incarnation, when human beings, who have just touched the fringe of the glorious truth that they are part of the Infinite Life, imagine themselves to be superior to all external means of grace, and symbols, and Sacraments. Jesus said, "The Father in Me doeth the works." He was the representative of the Originating Mind in all that He said and did, and this adds a peculiar fascination and solemnity to the incidents of the institution of the Eucharist.

The three years' ministry of tenderness and self-sacrifice were about to close, and, during that solemn time before the Crucifixion, in the quiet of those last hours, when voices were hushed and hearts were heavy with a sense of coming sorrow, when every word from His lips acquired an intenser emphasis and a deeper meaning, when His own, whom He loved unto the end, were round Him, and heart was twined with heart, " He took bread and blessed it, and said, 'Take, eat, this is My Body.' He took the cup, saying, 'Drink ye all of it, for this is My Blood.' " My visible Presence, which is a Sacrament, a specialization, of the " Personalness " of the Infinite Mind, is about to be removed, but there shall be a contact-point between us; I shall leave this ceremony as a Sacrament a specialization, of My invisible Presence, as My parting legacy, My ever-present hand-grasp out of the Infinite. And by the memory of that life of unrivalled beauty, by the memory of that last night of sorrow, the millions of Christendom, amongst them the highest human intellects, who have learnt to love that wondrous Being, even if they have not fully realized His Transcendent Majesty, have been constrained by impulse irresistible thus to obey His last command.

Now we are living in a time of great change in apprehension and ideal. Spiritual perceptions, confined in the past to a few mystics, are now more commonly opened, and new schools of thought are springing up around individual teachers. Ideally it is inspiring, practically it demands caution. There are an increasing number who have found their wings and are exchanging the narrowness of limitations for an illuminated universalism. They have rediscovered in the writings of Western Theosophists, such as Jacob Boehme, the truth of the Immanence of God, and they imagine themselves to be wholly independent of all external means of grace, oblivious of the fact that while their differentiated spirits are enclosed in the materialization of a physical body, the Universal Spirit will quicken them through material means. They absent themselves from the Blessed Sacrament, the central act of worship of the whole Catholic Church, not from a sense of unworthiness, quite the reverse, but from a sense of superiority. I desire respectfully to ask them a question.

Do you, who, by studying "higher thinking," have recognized the Immanence of Infinite Mind in all phenomena, ask what the Lord Jesus meant when He affirmed that bread and wine were His Body and Blood? Do you repeat the superficial materialistic question of the Jews, "How can this Man give us His flesh to eat?" Did you never consider the fact of "Philosophical Transubstantiation?" Obviously the specialization of Infinite Mind in Jesus could say of all phenomena, whether tree, flower, bread, or wine, " this is My body," and if, for a specific purpose, He Himself separated off any bit of nature, and impressed special significance upon it, it would become a sacrament, an " outward and visible sign," a " means whereby to receive," and to come into contact with, Himself.

If you start thinking from the incontrovertible philosophic inference that the Christ is the impersonation of the Logos, which is the Soul of the universe, it logically follows that to ignore sacraments, to consider yourself superior to sacraments, on the ground that you have recognized your oneness with Infinite Life, is to confess ignorance of one of the conditions of Infinite Life, which is the immense power that the forces in the invisible world exercise over the visible world. The visible world is thrilling with the universal cosmic mind, and a sacrament, authoritatively instituted, and rightly celebrated, is a divinely appointed method whereby the energies of the immanent cosmic mind are specialized, and brought into activity on the earth plane.

All thinkers will follow me when I remind you that the cosmic mind, which is intensely intelligent, is subconscious mind; that is, it has not initiative, but is keenly sensitive to suggestion. It is by subconscious mind that the bee makes its hexagonal cell, and the beaver his scientific dam, and the bower-bird in India her nest inpregnable to the snake. Not by purposeful, creative, initiative, but in response to suggestion; the suggestion originally of need, or desire, or fear; and by inheritance and race-memory the original suggestion becomes a race-habit which we call instinct. Now Jesus was the specialization of the Infinite Superconscious Mind, which is God. Therefore when He suggested anything to the cosmic subconscious mind, His suggestion was instantly adopted. That was why the fig-tree withered away, and why the nets on the Sea of Galilee were filled with fishes. When He took into His hands a Galilean loaf, and juice of the grape, and authoritatively suggested to the subconscious cosmic mind "This is My body," the elements did not change their nature, they were always His body, always manifestations of the Creative Logos, but they became His body and blood, His substance and life, in a new sense; they became, not symbolically only, but actually, the material means of conveying the grace which He had suggested. Now this I understand to be the effect of the consecration prayer upon the elements in the Holy Eucharist. The suggestion that the

Christ made to the cosmic subconsciousness, when in the upper chamber at Jerusalem He instituted the Eucharist, remains vital in His Church; it is continued influentially, and attached to the word, action, and intention, of His ordained representatives, who consecrate the elements. The substance that is changed in the bread and wine by the actions and the words spoken by the ordained minister, is not the substance of flour and water, and the juice of the grape. The substance, the *substantia*, that is changed is the functioning of the thought-form that lies behind the elements, the thought that made those portions of matter what they were. The Superconscious Mind, which is formative and creative, has suggested to the subconscious mind in the elements, which is sensitive and receptive, a new power, a new character, and they become vehicles of energies higher than those which habitually belong to them, and this is Philosophical Transubstantiation.

Everything in physical nature is what it is by reason of the immanence of a spiritual organism or mind-form which relates it to the Universal Mind. This mind-form, being sub-conscious, is instantly receptive of any impression given to it by the Universal Super-conscious Mind, and if the Omnipotent Superconscious Mind suggests to the spiritual organism immanent in any phenomenon of nature that its power of functioning is other than it appears to be, that, in its action, though not in its appearance, it immediately becomes.

It is evident that the Lord Jesus meant the Holy Eucharist to be the authorized ceremony in the due performance of which the world of sense and the world of spirit should touch and blend, and, as it were, overflow the one into the other.

St. Paul says that we " have come," not we shall come, " unto an innumerable company of angels, to the general assembly and Church of the first-born, to God the Judge of all, and to the spirits of just men made perfect." The Eucharist is the authoritative channel through which this glorious contact is made, and in the Eucharist the hearts of weary human beings, longing, hungering, for the beloved who have passed into the other dimension, reach for awhile from the seen into the unseen world and are able to say, without exaggeration, and with infinite soul-peace, " Therefore with Angels and Archangels, and with all the company of Heaven, we laud and magnify Thy glorious Name; evermore praising Thee, and saying Holy, Holy, Holy, Lord God of Hosts; Heaven and earth (invisible and visible) are full of Thy glory; Glory be to Thee, O Lord most High."

Then, again, the Eucharist is the act guaranteeing the Real Presence of the Objective Personal Christ. No one doubts that the Christ, as the Logos, is Omnipresent; but the Divine Lord knew that we cannot always live in full realization of our highest beliefs and ideals. He knew how great a blessing a guaranteed contact-point with Himself would be to us, and so He gave us the Holy Eucharist, not to make a Presence that was not there before, but specially to focus, at an agreed upon and specific moment, in an appointed and guaranteed ordinance, the eternal truth of the Universal Presence. In the Eucharist we consciously meet Him. We may use the power of our imagination to call up a form of Him before the mind's eye. As the Omnipresent Logos He is a diffused, universalized, divine abstraction; in the Eucharist He is specialized as a Person. I come to the Eucharist to meet Him, to worship Him, to speak to Him face to face.

Now one thought more. It is necessary for the recipient of the Eucharist to fulfil the conditions enabling the healing energy of the ceremonial to be brought into contact with the human soul. There is an atterance of St.

Paul which, because it is misunderstood, has frightened some from the Eucharist ; it suggests that " we eat and drink unworthily if we discern not the body." Now the " Body " which we are to " discern " to be worthy participants of the Eucharist is the human race. Humanity is the Body of God, the highest expression of Infinite Mind when He was attaining self-realization in objective phenomena. The quality that God was seeking to realize when He made humanity was Love. That fact suggests that individual man is not the highest manifestation of Infinite Mind, but that humanity is ; for the principle of love requires fellow human beings to be loved ; therefore the complete " Body " of God that we are to " discern " is not the individual but the human race, and the Eucharist was to be the witness of the solidarity of this Body, and of the personal obligation of each one towards it, so that a communicant " eats and drinks judgment to himself if he discern not the Body." Study the context and you will see that this is the interpretation. Want of unity, isolation, self-centredness, are what the Apostle is condemning. " I hear," he says, " that there are divisions among you " ; you are one Body, you are communicating unworthily if you discern not the Body, you have missed the meaning of the Eucharist if you regard human beings as isolated units. Humanity is the Body of the Infinite Creative Mind.

The condition, then, of a worthy partaking of Holy Communion is not only a hunger for close personal contact with the Christ, it is also a recognition of that mystic oneness that knits the race in which God has expressed Himself into a unity far closer than brotherhood.

The highest consideration that can influence the mind of man is that transcendent truth that humanity is the Body of God, and that God's life in man is the one basal principle of "Peace on earth and good will amongst men." When it obtains, as it must obtain, it will obliterate all chasms between man and man, between nation and nation, for men will know that God's full Christ, God's true Son, is not one man only, but the whole multitudinous race of men, of which race the Lord Jesus is the perfect, full-orbed, Archetypal specimen. How then can we, as individuals, qualify so as not to hinder the power of the Eucharist by wrong thinking? We cannot, alas, do much in the sphere of the universal. We cannot check the ruinous competition in armaments and ironclads and aeroplanes which threatens to bankrupt Europe. But we can carry out the principle in the sphere of the particular. We can school ourselves never to hate any one, to see our fellow-creatures after the spirit and not after the flesh ; at every Eucharist we can "discern the Body" by praying for every soul in the Church, by sending love thoughts, peace thoughts, all around ; and we can carry the thought over the border and claim that sweet fusing of the two worlds which makes the Holy Eucharist an assured meeting-place between ourselves and our beloved departed.

"Lord, where Thou art our beloved dead must be.
Unpierced as yet the Sacramental mist,
But we are nearest them and nearest Thee
At solemn Eucharist.

Lord, where Thou art our beloved dead must be,
And as with Thee what then their boundless bliss !
Till Faith be sight and Hope reality
Love's anchorage is This."

## THE PAST

**" That which hath been is now, and that which is to be hath already been, and God requireth that which is past."—ECCLES. iii. 15.**

RETROSPECT, I know, is futile and generally depressing, but it is almost inevitable on the last day of a year. The surface application of these words, " God requireth that which is past," needs no comment. They who think on the rudimentary plane, which is a very useful plane, and who avoid abstruse investigation, may take the words just as they stand, as a motto for the last day of one of those articulations of eternity that we call years. Memory, which is the sum of the images that experience forms in the mind, will do its chastening work, and fulfil for each one the declaration, " be sure thy sin will find thee out." Sin is the denial of sinfulness: " If we say we have no sin, we deceive ourselves, but if we confess our sin, He is faithful and just to forgive us our sin "; but to confess our sin, remember, is not merely to be whitewashed by the absolution of a priest, but to feel our wrong-doing, and hate it so bitterly as to be willing to die to be free from it. For practical purposes, for simplicity of statement, we might there leave the saying in Ecclesiastes.

But the words mean more than this. What is the past? Is it necessary for man to be dominated and terrorized by the past? Aristotle says, in his *Ethics*, book VI, "Of this alone is even God deprived, namely, of the power of making that which is past never to have been." Now is this true? I mean, is it true to the philosophic thinker? It seems to me that even our finite minds can cognize ways in which the past can be made "never to have been." The first is by carrying to its logical conclusion St. Paul's "dream-theory" of manifested human life. The gifted Editor of *The Seeker* once wrote a powerful article on St. Paul's dream-theory, which I enjoy, but cannot wholly endorse. But, if it is true, as Shelley says, "Peace, peace, he is not dead, he doth not sleep, he hath awakened from the dream of life"; if it is true, as Ruskin says, "We are all plunged into a languid dream, our eyes heavy, our ears closed"; or, as Sir Thomas Browne says in his *Religio Medici*, "We are all asleep in this world, the concepts of this life are mere dreams"; or, if we are to give full meaning to Paul's reiterated challenge, "awake thou that sleepest," then it is just possible that this life's painful experiences have no more reference to our true divine ego than the experiences of a dream have to our waking consciousness. Then, when we are living and thinking only on the plane of ordinary consciousness, sensitive only to mundane conditions and experiences, we are in dream-land, and all that complex formation of what Paul calls "the carnal mind," that totality of feeling and habit and mental images, inherited or self-engendered, which is the seat of error, superstition, materialism and fear, is not the real self but the dream self; and the "dream of life," though startlingly vivid, and intensely educative as a test and a warning, is not the sphere of reality, of permanence, of the real self. In an ordinary dream (I am not speaking of the rare occasions when the Divine Spirit uses a dream to send a message, as to Joseph, the husband of Mary), but in an ordinary dream, our actions are often such as the waking self repudiates with abhorrence; for the dream-self acts with certain faculties in abeyance, and the lower side of the consciousness is then uncontrolled by the higher. Now, waking from such a dream is an instantaneous passing from one plane of consciousness to another, and recognizing that the dream consciousness was unreal, and that the actions of the dream never happened. To awake breaks a chain of very vivid experiences which seemed intensely real; so real that they have a definite effect upon character; but to awake is to know that these experiences never really were, they only seemed to be; and on waking, one says: Thank God that was only a dream, a dream able to work in me a keen consciousness of the deadliness and bitterness of folly, of wrongdoing, and wrong thinking, but, thank God, that never happened. According to this theory awakened consciousness has done that which Aristotle said even God could not do, it has "caused that which is past never to have been."

Now it is a bold suggestion, I allow, but it is the legitimate corollary of Paul's deliberate severance of his true ego from his flesh and blood self, and his reiterated challenge to us to awake from sleep. It suggests that life, as we know it, with its follies and its failures, may be as unreal as a dream; that the real ego, hidden in the bosom of God, has committed none of the actions that we deplore; that, in that sense, they never have been, though dreaming them was educative, and though spiritual consciousness may not yet fully justify us in the deliberate disentangling of the real self from the authorship of evil deeds, as Paul so boldly did when he said, " It is not I, but sin that dwelleth in me," it should encourage us to force our conscious minds to awake from dreamland and claim our full inheritance in God ; to affirm again and again, " I am spirit, I am not my body " ; to ignore more and more the demands and conditions of the outer, material self, and to treat it, as Shakespeare says, as being " such stuff as dreams are made of." Then when we truly wake into spiritual consciousness here, or, through the experience that we call death, awake in the other sphere of being, we shall know that the past that we dread and deprecate is but " the baseless fabric of a dream."

But, to the thinker, the inspired utterance in Ecclesiastes suggests yet another contradiction to the dogmatic statement of Aristotle. The words in Ecclesiastes are, " that which hath been is now." Then, in reality, there is no past, it is all " now." The finite mind, thinking on the material plane, and full of inherited mental images, cannot grasp an everlasting " now " ; but there is no Time to Spirit, God is Spirit, Man is Spirit. The definition of spirit is, " I am," not I was, and I shall be, but " I am."

> "Never the spirit was born,
> The spirit shall cease to be never,
> Never was time it was not,
> End and beginning are dreams.

That is as true of you and me, as regards our real self, as it is of God. Then how can there be any past, in reality, otherwise than as a necessary educative illusion?

What is Time? The philosophic thinkers and writers all forbear to define Time. Immanuel Kant says: "Time is simply our way of being conscious of one thing going before, and another thing coming after, something else." Another metaphysician says: "Time is limited human perception whereby we think of things in succession." Another says: "Time is a subjective notion imposed by our perception in the representation of things."

You observe, all these philosophers assume that Time exists only in our thought, that all the accompaniments of experience connected with what we call Time have no more reality than the opinion we entertain of them. Things are what we think they are. Time is because we think it is; and why do we think it is? Because Originating Father-Spirit implanted the thought of duration into the human organism when He prepared the individual life-centres in which He expresses Himself, and we inherit the mental image, the race-thought, of duration from thousands of generations of ancestors, during which it has been intensified. That is why our bodies grow old and decay. The sub-conscious mind of every member of the race, always obedient to suggestion, adopts the suggestion of the duration of time, and works it out logically with such tenacity that, apart from its having been first suggested by the Creative Superconscious Mind, it becomes ineradicable. If this be so, and it must be so to spirit, then time, in the sense of past, present and future, is but a department of human intelligence, working educatively, under a law initiated by the Originating Spirit, the consciousness of which law we shall lose when we awake to full spiritual knowledge.

For this thought the writer of Ecclesiastes is responsible. Is there value in it ? There is ; it saves you from the dominance of the past, from fruitless mourning over past actions Twenty years ago you did this or that, you lost this or that opportunity, it is buried in the past, you can't undo it, the burden of it is intolerable. Ecclesiastes says : " Twenty years ago ! There is no twenty years ago to spirit, there is no time to spirit, you can obliterate it at this moment, as if you committed it now, to-day, by intense mental concentration upon reality, upon your inseverability from God, upon the all-surrounding, indwelling Divine Love."

Doubtless you cannot touch adverse conditions that may seem to you to have arisen from your action; to your material senses you cannot alter what you think has already happened; but you can flood the whole incident, the whole memory, with the high and noble thoughts of spiritual consciousness; you can place yourself in tune with the Infinite, you can realize your oneness with God, you can mentally disentangle yourself, and any you may think you have injured, from those deeds that seem to be in the past, and say: "All that is real is God, He is all of me, He is all of everybody, I and they are individualized parts of God, there is no time to God, therefore there is no past to God, that which hath been is now."

Possibly neither of these thoughts, though they both contradict Aristotle, will really hold the imagination. The inherited race-belief in the passage of time is too strong, we are all necessarily dominated by it. What attitude of mind, then, do I suggest for the average man, in which category I include myself, on the last day of a year? I would say, don't look backward or forward, but look inward and outward. Steady yourself mentally, "Be still and know."

Find the Originating Spirit, the Divine Love, within you, where He certainly is, and around you like an atmosphere of light and life. Find "the secret place of the Most High." Pray the Universal Father-Soul to reveal Sonship, to reveal the Christ nature, that is, to reveal Himself, in you. Learn to know that you live in a Presence, and that a Presence lives in you; claim its manifestation, and, for your needs, draw directly from the Universal Divine Love; place your thoughts deliberately under His guidance; do not despise or ignore existing mundane conditions, with their responsibilities; the material plane is your plane of action, its details are your education, but do not consider this plane either real or permanent. Remember that Originating Spirit, Who brought everything into being from His Own substance, is the root of your individual life, and that He is "the Power that worketh in you both to will and to do."

To strive after this attitude means wrestling against wrong mentality; the very fact that you are wrestling will reconstitute your character, and readjust your relations with external facts. This thought-wrestle will come into manifestation in a purer, stronger, less selfish life. It will lift you above the tyranny of second causes. Second causes are the nightmare of material existence. In second causes human life often seems to be at the mercy of blind and reckless chance. Spiritual consciousness knows better. Your affirmation, even before it is fully grasped by your intuition, is "God is all, and all is God, and God is Love, Truth, Wisdom, and Goodness, and in Him I live and move and have my being." Second causes are well enough for babes. A child strikes itself against something, and the nurse, to dry its tears, beats the object for hurting the child, and to the baby mind the problem is solved. It knows not that the bruise was a detail of the operation of the most majestic law of the Universe, the law of gravitation, "the law that moulds a tear and preserves the earth a sphere." When you begin to know God as Universal Divine Love, you are free from the tyranny of second causes; you know that life, with its apparently insoluble problems, is inhabited, ensphered, penetrated, overshadowed by the majestic law of the Omnipotent Creative Spirit, who is immanent in all, and Whom Jesus taught us to address as "Our Father, which art in heaven."

And what are we, average men, to do with our past? We feel that we cannot rest in Paul's "dream theory," or in the "no Time" theory of Ecclesiastes; we are dominated by the irrevocability of the past. There have been perhaps, some cowardly defeats under temptation, we can't forget them, "the remembrance of them is grievous unto us, the burden of them is intolerable"; our increasing knowledge of the perfect love and goodness of the Father-Spirit smites the soul with the cry, "So ignorant was I and foolish, like as it were a beast before Thee."

I cannot recall those falls, or re-live them, or forget them. Those hours, "*transeunt et imputantur*"; or, as Shakespeare says, "I wasted time, and now time wastes me." Now, without either Paul's theory, or the theory of Ecclesiastes, there is a sense in which we can say there is in reality no past. Why not? Because the past is in me, it is myself, what I am to-day is my past incorporated into character. The question is not what I did, but what I am. Look at an oak tree of 100 years old, which has been sawn through. Mark its annual growth circles, clearly delineated in its bulk; those growth circles are its past; and they are itself. Each man is, in a sense, his past, but he can do what the oak tree cannot do, he can obliterate and outlive those growth rings, and he can do it now, to-day. Paul says, "Be ye transformed by the renewing of your mind." When you are transformed the past is gone. To be "transformed by the renewing of your mind" is resolutely to turn your whole being to God as a flower turns to the sunshine. It is to say: "Infinite Creative Majesty, Omnipotent Divine Spirit, I place myself unequivocally, without reservation, into harmony with Thy divine purpose for me. I will suffer no image to enter my mind but that of Thy perfected Will in my own personality. I hereby deliberately disentangle my real self from the record of the past, and I affirm myself to be Thy child."

Most of us will hear the great Westminster clock strike twelve to-night; let this thought be first of the New Year, begin to think it the moment the clock has ceased striking: "God is with me, God is with me, and God is Love." Immanuel, God with us. That is the message of Christmas Day of which to-day is the Octave. On the Octave of Christmas we once more publicly express our adoration of the revelation of the Incarnation by kneeling when we repeat in the Nicene Creed the words, "and was made man." They are wonderful words of life. What more could Divine Love do to assure us that He was with us than come to us under the forms and limitations of a human personality. God is with us, to know it is to know the secret of the Lord. Look at the inscription on Wesley's tomb in the Abbey. When he lay dying, and his words were almost indistinguishable, one sentence burst with clear emphasis from his lips: "The best of all is God is with us." Yes, God was with him; he may have made many mistakes, the best men make many mistakes, mistake is God's educator, but God had been always with him, and was with him then, as He will be with you and me, at the moment of death.

The coming year is a book of which the pages are uncut. We know not what awaits us. Life is not easy, whether it be in the temptations of commerce, the duties of a household, the activities of manual labour, or ministering to sick bodies or perplexed souls. It is an unspeakably blessed comfort to know, really to know, that the Father-Spirit is always with us, and that He will overshadow and inspire the life of His child.

I should like my last word to be this: Let us never deflect from that standard of assurance of our Divine origin. "Now are we the sons of God," says St. John. Then our Father's nature must be within us, and not to know it is to be ignorant of the true philosophy of life. Once more I quote those inspired lines by James Rhoades—

" Again that voice that on my listening ears
Falls like star-music filtering through the spheres.
Know this, O man, sole root of sin in thee
Is not to know thine own divinity."